Money Wisdom

Money Wisdom

Creating the Vibrational Energy of Wealth in any Economy

Karen L. Garvey

INTENT, LLC

Money Wisdom

Creating the Vibrational Energy of Wealth in any Economy

(originally Wyce's Money Book ©2008)

Printed in the United States of America

INTENT, LLC

373 Nesconset Highway #125
Hauppauge, New York 11788

ISBN 978-0-9764663-2-1

Acknowledgement

I'd like to thank those who have shared with me insights into what my books mean to them.

The purpose of my books is to provide as many people as possible with information that may increase their level of awareness and it is a privilege for me to be able to do so.

CONTENTS

Introduction

Money Wisdom (originally released as Wyce's Money Book) is the second book in **THE ANSWERS** series. For those who have read the first book, **THE ANSWERS to your questions about life**, the process behind "receiving" this book needs no introduction; however, for others who are not familiar with **THE ANSWERS**, let me give a brief insight into the development of this series.

After I realized my ability to communicate with souls without physical bodies, I found the information from these souls to be so profound that I sought to develop this skill to my greatest capacity. The "conversations" that I had gave refreshing perspectives about virtually any earth matter – perspectives which were enlightening about why we are here, our eternal journeys, the reasons behind earth circumstances, and how we can enjoy happier lives. As I learned more from this other realm, the energy realm, I discovered fascinating insights into topics as diverse as "how do humans affect weather patterns," to "how do humans create their reality in the earth realm."

One skill that developed quickly for me was the ability to channel material from souls in the energy realm. My first channeled project was the book, **THE ANSWERS to your questions about life**. Many readers have provided feedback, sharing ways in which the book enabled them to discover how to be happier and live more fulfilling lives. I (along with the entities who developed the material in the book) am grateful that **THE ANSWERS** is significantly assisting others. While continuing their quest to increase the level of awareness and therefore happiness of humanity, my guides have provided this, the second book in **THE ANSWERS** series. As **THE ANSWERS** presented intense insights into our lives' purpose, **Money Wisdom** provides original insights into money's purpose in our earth lives.

Although it often seems that there are no new concepts on earth, this book proves otherwise. The book's definitions of money and its usage are revolutionary. The fundamental understanding of these ideas acts as a springboard for individuals to grasp how they have been effectively or ineffectively incorporating their relationship with money into their lives. Uncovering these principles allows readers to integrate changes that enable them to have completely abundant and prosperous lives.

Periodically, the book refers to an exercise that was delineated in **THE ANSWERS to your questions about life.** Although there is great value in reading **THE ANSWERS** prior to reading this book, it is not essential. For readers who want to enjoy the usefulness of **Money Wisdom** without first reading **THE ANSWERS**, you may email a request for the exercise.[1] The excerpt will be emailed to you so that you may realize the full benefit of this book.

If you have a question about life, ask. When you pose a question quietly to yourself or aloud, you may be surprised to sense the answer from a higher source. If you'd prefer a more "earthly" form of an answer, you may contact us at

---

1 Send email request to **exercise@TheAnswersUnlimited.com**

www.TheAnswersUnlimited.com. Questions or input from readers often lead to new areas of conversation between me and the entities, and you never know when your inquiry will lead to the development of a new book or audio program from the entities.

My guides continually plan new conveyances of valuable information. The material is limitless, just as our soul's potential is without limit. I enjoy my role in providing this information and look forward to continuing this journey with you.

In the Beginning

Fortunately, fortune is rather easy to come by. It has become ever so complicated and convoluted by misconceptions and false ideas, but it is fundamentally simple when these mis-ideas are stripped away.

As long as we focus.

And focus is the key. You cannot enjoy the rich knowledge of matters of earth abundance and material wealth if you half-heartedly pay attention to the components and influences of such matters. Yet, that's pretty much what people do all the time. They half-heartedly pay attention to those matters they supposedly want. You cannot achieve a "want" or a goal without diligent focus.

If you have not yet experienced the abundance in your life that you would like, you can learn by your missteps as much as from your successes. See, the absence of success is often a stronger indication of what will work than what actually works. Sounds contrary, yes? However, often if success comes too readily, there is no FOCUS on what brought it about and, therefore, no way to duplicate it once gone.

Karen acts a conduit to receive the material for this book. All that exists in the eternal journey may have been forgotten on a day-to-day basis, but it does not prevent you from tapping into the river of universal of knowledge, either through your own intuition or through Karen's access. Understanding that you are interconnected with all that exists can help you to recognize that you are not alone in your moments of defeat, in your moments of discovery, and in your moments of celebration. Throughout this workbook, we will share with you little anecdotes about life in the energy realm. Perhaps our stories will trigger your own memories about your journey as a soul before you leaped into physical existence.

First, let us tell you the most basic difference between reality created among those on earth and those souls without a physical vehicle. The prime difference is that here, we KNOW that we create our reality and we do so willingly and brilliantly. On earth, a type of birth amnesia occurs – perhaps as a learning tool for the soul's growth, and this amnesia prevents earthlings (most earthlings) from remembering that they create their reality with their thoughts.

We will attempt, through this workbook, to remind you how to create your reality in the area of abundance and material wealth. It's not very hard. Earthlings often overcomplicate or over-think matters, but if you give these exercises an earnest try, you will likely realize results that appeal to you within a reasonable amount of time.

Let's talk about "reasonable amount of time." The basis of knowledge on earth about quantum physics teaches that there is no such thing as time. This is true. There is no such thing as time. The universe *wants* to provide you with all that you desire, but since time does not exist in universal terms, the time frame in which this process can occur is not quantifiable. Why are we telling you this? Because if your results are not occurring as quickly as you would like, then we ask that you please be patient a bit longer. YOU do not define the time frame; the universe will comply as it can within the amount of time necessary to comply.

We must state the assumption that you have read **THE ANSWERS to your questions about life** by now. **THE ANSWERS** book is the precursor to the exercises in **MONEY WISDOM**. Alone, neither can propel you as "quickly" (hmmm … didn't we just contradict ourselves?) as together they both can (and by "quickly," we mean "effectively.") Towards the end of **THE ANSWERS**, an exercise is delineated that provides the basis for what is to come in this book. This exercise can be effective for altering or taking charge of your reality in many areas, not just wealth, but this book will focus simply on wealth as an opportunity to strengthen your focus on one desire.

The next portion of this book is meant to enlighten you about matters of money that you may not be aware. The most studied student of economics or the wealthiest venture capitalist cannot know these next matters of money unless they are immensely intuitive or never experienced earth amnesia (the disconnect from eternal memories).

What is Money?

Think about your answer to the question before you read on. What is money? Is it a product used in the exchange of goods and services at an agreed upon rate? We're seeking your "textbook" response here. From an economic and practical standpoint, how do you define money?

Is money necessary?

Wow – we could answer that question in all kinds of ways and it could probably lead to a book of its own.

What else do you know about money? We want you to really think about it from a different perspective than you are accustomed to thinking. How much is too much? How much is enough? If it is necessary, what did man do before they conjured up the idea of money? Even beyond the concept of bartering or swapping seashells, what did mankind do before they had money?

Well, to be certain they maintained autonomy. They self-reliantly provided for all the items that they needed or wanted, from their shelter to their food to their items of luxury. Could you succeed under such a system? It is rather easy to understand why a semblance of trade or bartering began to evolve so that people could acquire a larger variety of goods than they could readily create or gather or produce.

What freedom humans began to experience when bartering or trading became commonplace. Suddenly, there were goods available for "purchase" that had never been previously attainable. A man who shepherded sheep could swap a few for leather wares or cooking utensils. The world began to open up. As long as a person could grow or produce or attain something of value to others, he or she could access a wide array of other products.

Life just kept getting better and better, for eventually a clever genius came up with the idea of exchanging a third product as payment for the goods and services. Now people could rate the value of their items and exchange them for a greater multitude of items than a simple barter arrangement would allow. Shops started to pop up. As long as everyone agreed upon the relative worth of items, money began to be exchanged, extending the freedom of choice for all involved.

Money affords a great amount of freedom.

Can you imagine going back to pre-money times? What are you good at? How much of it could you attain or create to exchange for other things that you wanted? Suppose you own a pizza shop. How many pizzas would you need to give to SONY in exchange for a High Definition TV?

How many chicken Parmesan heroes are needed for the bank to let you borrow several hundred thousand dollars for a house? Speaking of houses, how many bottles of soda would you need to furnish your local government with for your annual property tax payment?

What a complicated mess life would be without money. We can likely agree that money is a good thing and affords a great amount of freedom. So what happened to complicate the concept of money so greatly since the earliest times of its exchange?

It is not just growth and sophistication or an increase in available goods or services that complicated money. It's more than that. Think back again to pre-money days. Perhaps a tailor exchanged his handcrafted dresses and suits in exchange for the wares that he required and desired. Now suppose he made four dresses, but only exchanged three, holding onto the fourth for a rainy day. Then he made seven suits and offered four for exchange, keeping three for unforeseen future circumstances. What if the time and fabric it took to make the not-offered items caused him to be short in goods that he could exchange for all he wanted.

In the same town, a farmer began to offer only some of his cattle for exchange. By holding back many, his need to feed and care for the growing herd grew, but his exchange quantity did not. By holding back, he eventually wound up with a bunch of old cows not worth exchanging for anything. Yet, people today hoard money all the time. Why do they do that? Some people borrow cows from others and use those in exchange for what else they want. Others, still, can't raise enough cows to keep their basic necessities covered.

What happened to the usage of money between the simple exchange days till now?

A lot happened between then and now, and a fundamental

understanding of what occurred can help you to adjust your relationship with money towards a more prosperous one.

On earth, when people exchanged goods and services through bartering and trading, they focused on what they wanted and believed it was possible to get. If they wanted to "save up" for a new cooking pot, they, perhaps, planted a few more rows of corn for eventual exchange. There was simplicity in the barter system because there were relatively few items available for trade.

Suddenly, a "wealthy" man, one who had more sheep available for exchange, began to have more options. Imported items became available. The variety of wares presented grew and grew. So did envy. So did the feeling of lack among those who did not have what others did. Self-worth began to be equated to what a man owned. Owning more became desirable and people began to assign value to the quantity that a person owned. This visibility in ownership of wealth became covert as money replaced the barter system. No longer would one know for certain what a man owned, as money allowed for secrecy that sheep did not.

Money transformed itself from being a tool for attaining and exchanging goods to a complex concept integrated with emotions and feelings. The power of money began to take on a life of its own as the wares available for purchase increased daily. Money provided an unprecedented means to hoard, to hide, or to exchange.

You may be confused at this point, supposing that a man who owned more sheep was certainly considered wealthier than a man who owned fewer sheep during the days of barter. To a certain extent, yes, but when few goods were available for trade, there were just so many sheep that a man could own that still had incremental value for him. Also, ultimately, the item any one person used to exchange for goods was effectively "money," with the primary difference being a lack of ability to hide one's wealth. This distinction becomes relevant as we continue our discussion.

The days of old were simple in that there existed little variation on the theme of wanting, believing, attaining, and creating reality. The variety of parameters that could obscure this basic living instinct was limited. Money complicated the direct relationship that humans had with creating their reality. Does this mean that without money all people existed in perfect harmony with their needs and wants being met? No, of course not. Drought, famine, illness, and the like still existed, but the influence was more direct – the cause and effect almost more natural before money entered into the framework of existence.

The idea of money introducing the capacity to be hidden is significant overtly and metaphorically as well. The "game" changed when people were able to hide what they owned. Power shifted. Sometimes, the person with less could act as though he had more and shift his stature in the eyes of others. Likewise, a miserly man could have excess abundance so well hidden that he was treated charitably or ostracized by others.

Metaphorically, the ability to hide money, or wealth, symbolized the hiding of the significant power that money held. Money itself, almost an emotional intangible in comparison to goods that were previously traded, began to accumulate the emotions that exchange previously held, plus, began to attract new emotional levels of importance that did not exist during the exchange system.

This concept is a difficult concept to grasp, so we will now take you forward to the current emotional make-up that exists in relation to money.

As the shift from exchange of goods to the third-party use of money took place, a tremendous power and significance grew with the growth of the usage of money. Now, owning money became important. Because it is portable and concealable, people began to desire more money than they needed, more money than they presently owned, and more money than their neighbors possessed. Money itself became the symbol for prosperity, freedom, and power. It also became a symbol for greed, charity, and exploitation. Depending on its usage and its owner, it became a tool of influence; a lack of money had the power to influence others in certain ways, whereas prosperity in money allowed different kinds of influence.

The subtle shift in the power of the unit of exchange for goods and services began to attract the energy of human thinking, creating, and believing more than the direct goods had during barter times. As this shift grew stronger, people began to emote directly with money instead of emoting about the purchasing power of money.

Here is where life changed almost completely, at least in industrialized nations. The more emotionally charged money in its own right became, the more it became a vehicle for human interactions on every level. Eventually, especially in the past several hundred years, the accumulation or attainment of money became, to many, more important than any other aspect of living.

We will now describe money to you in a way that you have never understood it. You will forever think differently about its true purpose in the universe and it will greatly affect your ability to successfully bring in the wealth that you desire.

So, What Is Money?

You believe money is real. Almost all earthlings believe money is real, but it is not. It is an illusion. Most everything on earth is an illusion, but money is more mysterious and intriguing in that it is highly regarded as containing truth. It does no such thing. Money is illusory and false as well.

At this point, you likely recognize that money is not what it seems; money has false emotionally charged ideas and expectations associated with it and, as is all things on earth, money is an illusion.

So what is money, really? Money is a vehicle on earth for humans to express love. Every interaction concerning money is an expression of love in one form or another. As you may recall from THE ANSWERS, the purpose of life is to love, to create, and to learn, in that order. There are no exceptions. Money is quite simply one of the tools that humans use in this quest, with its primary overlaying characteristic providing the means to give, receive, and express love. From the springboard of love, money ventures widely into the areas of creating and learning. Since money dances so heavily among all three of these primary purposes in life, you can imagine how significant its usage has become.

How does money act as a vehicle in the area of love? First, let's identify the primary areas in which humans have a capacity to love:

- Love of self
- Love of select others

- Love of all others or love of humanity
- Love of animals
- Love of plants
- Love of earth (such as water, air, fire, soil)
- Love of physical existence beyond earth (stars, planets, galaxies, etc.)
- Love of inanimate objects
- Love of concepts and ideas
- Love of senses and stimuli sensed

Virtually any other type of love that you can think of falls within these categories or within an overlap of these categories. Within these categories, the use of money as an expression of love is endless. Let us illustrate with some examples.

A person grows up with an extremely stingy parent. The strident control over money that the parent exercises has little to do with need; the family has abundance. When this child grows up, he is likely to develop an extreme in his use of money as a result of the family patterns of behavior. Some possible outcomes:

- He may decide, on some level, that generosity is a more rewarding use of money than hoarding and thus give generously to others.
- He may try to overcome a lack of feeling self-worth based on the miserliness of his parent by hoarding or becoming miserly himself.
- He may find himself in a state of scarcity as a result of disdaining the distorted use of money that he became accustomed to.

First, let us acknowledge that the parent used money in a way to express love. By holding money back from loved ones, he may have been expressing his view of their worth, or outwardly demonstrating his love or lack of love. He may have been expressing self-love by overcoming a feeling of lack through the accumulation of money. He may have experienced low self-esteem that he compensated for by making money a tool in which others could demonstrate their love by acting within conditions that the money holder set forth.

We'll elaborate with some examples to further your understanding. Suppose this man, we'll call him Henry, had tons of money, more than he could ever use in his lifetime, and he also had low self-esteem. Such a set of conditions is ripe for a person to use money to gain control over the way others interact with him. With his lack of self-love, Henry created clever ways to cause people to "need" him. Through his stinginess, he caused his children and others to prove themselves to him in order to be compensated through matters of money. If his child displeased him, he could withdraw material expressions of approval. This tool is effective in guaranteeing that those wanting access to his money would behave in the way he desired. By using money in this regard, Henry could continue to live with low self-esteem by bringing people to him. He did not have to be concerned about his lovableness. He did not have to be concerned with his character. He did not have to look inwardly for ways to improve his relationships. Money acted as the vehicle that he manipulated to ensure others would be around; therefore, on some level, he would feel loved.

Let's go deeper into this example. Henry has three children: Mary, Betsy, and Tim. Betsy knows that she will not get any financial rewards if she displeases her father. She grows up wanting his love and recognizes on some level that her father shows his love materially, so she learns to take actions, speak, and even think according to his wishes. As such, he "controls" her; he even controls her willingness to think independently.

Down the road, she makes some "mistakes" in her father's eyes. He withdraws his expression of approval [actually unconditional love] by withdrawing financial rewards. Big dramas are created within her world. She fails to recognize that her dad is manipulating her out of his own unknown fear of being unworthy of her love, so the money is not the primary focus in times of strife. The focus for Betsy becomes, "What can I do to make him love me again?" The process is torturous for her, but she usually succeeds in behaving in a way that pleases him once again and she is financially or materially rewarded. The pattern of money being used as a vehicle to express or elicit an expression of love continues. Neither person is free. Henry is not free to be loved for himself and Betsy is not free to make her own choices based on what she wants throughout her life.

What is the outcome in this situation? Well, think down the road farther. Eventually, Henry reaches his final years. Suppose he loses his funds to illness or other circumstance. Betsy has spent her entire life living in accordance with her father's manipulations and, in the end, she doesn't realize much inheritance because it is lost.

Is she free? No. She can now begin to move away from the controls that he held over her or she can become embittered by the lack of inheritance. In either case, it is challenging for Betsy to understand the unconditional receipt or expression of love because they were distorted through her father's machinations.

Of course there are a million other probabilities that may have ensued within these parameters, but this illustration is a common one. Had Henry died with his fortune intact, perhaps Betsy would have felt loved as she received his inheritance. But, nevertheless, her control over her freedom would have been sacrificed without her ever having received the unconditional love she had coveted.

Mary, on the other hand, is a little less susceptible to her father's manipulations. Somehow, perhaps because she has fewer layers than Betsy, she innately knows that "kissing butt" is the way to get what she wants. She wants the material rewards and she wants the peace that comes with falling within his good graces. Mary develops manipulative tools of her own to maintain some freedom as well as get what she wants. She portrays herself as the ideal daughter according to his standards while she lives however she chooses. Carefully, she avoids getting caught when she falls outside of his "rules."

> **Money is a tool available on earth to assist humans along their growth paths.**

Once again, money is successful in getting what it is Henry believes he wants – children who act the way he wants and come around [thus indicating their love of him] to attain the material rewards for behaving the way he wants.

As you can begin to see, the whole idea of "love" becomes convoluted when money enters as a third party expression of love. Neither the giver nor the receiver learns what the true heartfelt expression of love entails.

Let's talk about Tim. Tim has a fiery soul. He cannot tolerate manipulations of any sort as his deep level of awareness protects him from any influence that may compromise his freedom.

Tim makes choices that are based on what he wants, often not to the liking of Henry. As a result, he's punished, or love is withdrawn, through Henry's control over money. He will not express, in a material way, satisfaction for Tim when Tim displeases him. As a result, Tim and Henry experience a tremendous amount of confusion about whether or not the other loves him. This confusion can be expressed as anger, rebellion, sadness, and even depression. See the power money has?

We want you to think even further about the endless ramifications that expressing love through money may have in this example. We will oversimplify the following illustration so that you may understand the far-reaching impact that money can have as a vehicle of expressing love.

Suppose all three children are gay. Imagine also that Henry is not open-minded, tolerant, or at all accepting of homosexuality. How do you suppose each person will deal with his or her gayness? A highly probable outcome is that Betsy will not admit her gayness, even to herself, for this falls outside of the comfort zone that pleasing her father gives her. Perhaps she marries. Can this union be a true soul-to-soul expression of love if Betsy is truly hiding her gayness? The couple may have a decent relationship, or perhaps not, but do you think the possibility exists that Betsy can express the unconditional love for her husband that she may have otherwise expressed for a female mate?

It is likely that Mary will live life expressing her true sexuality, but she will hide it from her father. Here we have a half-on, half-off ability to express love freely or to live freely by choice. Think about the day-to-day conflicts that arise as this matter remains hidden. How is Mary's expression of love for her mate compromised? How is her love of self affected?

Now, Tim, you may well imagine, lives openly. The consequence of his openness may be complete annihilation from the family, exile from portions of the family, or the reprieve of being "allowed" to be present at family gatherings with no love through money expressed towards him. How would each of these outcomes affect Tim's ability to express unconditional love to his mate, his sisters, his father, or himself? The possibilities are endless, but the true, uncorrupted ability to innately express unconditional love freely will be compromised to some degree or another.

We can follow this thread forever. The possible impact that using money as an expression of love has is infinite. In this scenario, money was used in a "closed" way. By "closed," we mean that love was not expressed in a free and open way. Think abut your energy when you are open. How do you feel? Think about your energy when you are closed. How do you feel? When you can imagine the differences in these feelings, you can begin to feel the power that money holds as a vehicle to express love.

We want to diverge for a moment. It's impractical to think that by reading the words, "money is simply a vehicle for the expression of love," that you can readily apply the value of this concept to your personal life. This concept will likely be new to each reader. There is little or no backup information on earth that will expound upon the simplicity, complexity, and usefulness of this concept. For this reason, we will explain and illustrate the idea more fully with the hope that you can grasp the benefits of this knowledge and apply it to your life. We also believe that you will be able to assess the actions of loved ones, the actions of neighbors, friends, townships, corporations, governments, and world leaders through this lens in order to develop an understanding of the significant manner in which money is simply a tool available on earth to assist humans along their growth paths.

Any radical new idea takes time to digest and replace common thoughts. Allow yourself time to apply the real concept of what money is and you will be rewarded in many ways. First, expect your tolerance of others' actions to expand. Secondly, expect your opinion of yourself to soften and strengthen: soften in relation to forgiving yourself for the perhaps unsatisfying relationship with money you presently hold, and strengthen your belief that you will now be able to create the wealth and prosperity that you desire. As your ability continually improves, your esteem in the area of creating wealth, and therefore, your self-esteem, will improve as well.

Let's get back to examples of how humans use money to

express love.

For the purpose of this next fictitious illustration, we will not give details about the participant's past experiences or his current feelings of self-love or love of others. Let's look simply at the details of his present actions.

A man, let's call him Jake, reads an article about the diminishing population of a rare bird that we'll call the Umbro. The article ignites his passion and he feels compelled to learn more. His research uncovers that the bird is near extinction as the result of the cumulative actions of humans continually threatening the Umbro's food source and land supply.

He sends a check to the SAVE THE UMBRO foundation. What has happened here? Jake makes a choice about the use of his money based on love. He chose to love himself by dedicating money to a cause he felt worthy. He is loving himself through this expenditure by allowing a visceral display of his compassion and kind-heartedness. In his belief system, a person who relishes the ongoing propagation of the myriad species on earth is a good person. A person who supports a threatened species with the aim of allowing the species to survive and perhaps thrive is a good person. Through his actions, he is also demonstrating a love for nature, a love for the "idea" that all created creatures have the right to continue their existence. He is indicating a love for the idea that obliteration of any natural species on earth is an injustice to the species and to humanity and to the globe in general. He is showing love for the animal kingdom in general and for the Umbro specifically.

He is also demonstrating love though a parallel emotion, hope. He is hopeful that his contribution can help remedy the actions of the people who are threatening the species. This hope is a reflection of his love for the possibility that mankind can correct harmful actions. To state this concept broadly, he is expressing love for the spirit of mankind – with the underlying, subconscious belief that man has the best interests of the earth and all its creatures at the core of its existence.

Now, we can view this same simple act of sending the check from an entirely different perspective – from the viewpoint of a lack of love. Suppose, when Jake reads the article, he's not feeling particularly happy with himself. Also, he is basically intolerant of others and has a generalized lack of faith in people's ability to "do the right thing." By writing the check, he is expressing love. He is attempting to use this act to feel better about himself or, in other words, to express self-love in an effort to alleviate his diminished feeling of self-worth. He is also expressing love, or lack thereof, for humans by using his money to reinforce his belief that people are not capable of doing the right thing. His money will help assuage the damage thoughtless people have created because he is good and worthy.

Through either scenario, we can see that relinquishing money is an act that expresses love [or a lack of love]. This one seemingly simple deed of sending the check to the foundation contained many subconscious [actually unconscious] opportunities to give and receive love.

We say "unconscious" because when we awaken to an

enlightened perspective, we become fully aware of our actions, their cause and consequence. Typically, however, people on earth remain unconscious about the reasons they behave the way they do. Their reason for being on earth, or their "quest," largely dictates the actions that they will take. The closer they are connected to their quest, the more positive their actions will be, and the further they separate from their intended quest, the less positive their actions will be.

The idea that money is a vehicle for the expression of love is called a "universal truth." A universal truth is incontrovertible, cannot be disproved, and cannot become "unknown" within a soul that makes its discovery. For example, if a woman operates primarily through the emotion of hate, when she discovers that love feels better, feels right, and provides positive outcomes, she has unearthed a universal truth. She cannot unlearn this truth. She may, out of the endearing human trait called "habit," continue to act hatefully, but the truth about the value of love cannot become unknown.

Universal truth is the avenue to satisfaction on earth in every area.

The idea that money is a vehicle for the expression of love is so powerful and true, that we will dedicate more illustrations to the concept in order for you to comprehend its significance.

Let's talk about greed. Greed is an exaggerated expression of love, primarily a lack of love. Greed, as we intend to use the word for this discussion, implies miserliness and hoarding.

What, in terms of love, is going on within a greedy person? A typical portrayal of a greedy person is one who is not emotionally connected to the outcome of his behavior. There is a component of indignation, self-righteousness, or entitlement. Overtly greedy people are often unable to connect emotionally with the consequence or pain that their actions may cause others.

The act of greediness is externally regarded as the act of a narcissistic person, or one who thinks great things about himself, when in fact it is primarily a veil to hide a profound lack of self-love. Let us illustrate.

A boy, Billy, grows up with an emotionally detached father. The father has amassed great wealth, but rarely shares his fortune with others. He is miserly and controls the action of others by doling out sums of money as "rewards" for approved behavior. He also projects an air of self-importance, as many wealthy people do.

In Billy's youth, the idea of money became convoluted as his father demonstrated grossly exaggerated attitudes towards its accumulation, its importance, and its usage. He also experienced a connection between his lovability and his receipt of money from his dad. In a perfect world, he would easily sort out the misinformation that he received and grow up developing a perfect relationship with money, but most often, misinformation in youth profoundly affects one's belief system in later years.

Billy grows up. He unconsciously believes that he must accumulate large sums of money in order to demonstrate his worthiness, so he sets out to do so. He also believes that money should be used to express satisfaction or dissatisfaction with people's actions. Already, without independently thinking about money from an unemotional perspective, he has strongly influenced ideas about how to love himself and how to love others through the use of money.

Suppose Billy opens a factory. How do you think his employees will be treated? Do you believe that they will be the best-paid in the industry? Do you think that their work environment will be the most aesthetic and comfortable? Already entrenched in a belief system that encourages greediness, Billy will likely expend the bare minimum necessary on employee comforts and wages. He will feel entitled to keep every penny earned that he can possibly keep. Interestingly, as his wealth grows, his self-esteem does not. Although outwardly he appears confident or even pompous, the appearance is an illusion. The accumulation of money masks his lack of self-love, but he has learned to appear confident because his belief system dictates he is worthy since he is wealthy.

Look at the misbeliefs that you were exposed to as a child, not only from your parents, but also from your religion, your government, or your education.

In this example, Billy is accumulating money (as a vehicle for the expression of love) in an attempt to love himself. He learned early on that a "lovable" person had money. He learned that to earn money meant you were worthwhile. His father's cheapness repeatedly indicated that if Billy was good, he was financially rewarded by some material expression of approval from his dad. Therefore, he began to believe that money itself was the reward … the expression of approval, or the receipt of love, was not.

And so it goes. Of course, the next step in understanding money as a vehicle for the expression of love in this example is to look at the reverse outcome.

It was likely that Billy would grow up to be greedy, but it was not inevitable. There are an infinite number of possible outcomes to any one person's life circumstances. Two people with nearly identical upbringings will not necessarily have the same belief structure as they mature.

In our quest to develop according to our souls' intent, we may choose the earth plane as a wonderful laboratory. With the vehicles of time and space available on earth as learning tools, earth provides souls with an ability to experiment or focus on small tasks. For example, suppose your intent or your quest was to increase your self-love. Here, in the energy realm, bliss is so natural a state that driving towards greater bliss is sometimes not compelling. By leaping into a physical life, the drive towards attaining bliss compels the soul to engage in the minutia of discovery and experimentation.

In Billy's case, his quest may have compelled him to discover his ability to love himself through greed, but he also could have followed an opposite route to attain this knowledge. He could have opted to demonstrate or grow self-love through generosity.

The "choices" of how to experiment with knowledge on

earth are not conscious decisions until universal truth is discovered and embraced. Since Billy was unaware of the detriment greediness had to his ability to meet his soul's intent, he unconsciously used this vehicle as an opportunity to expand his awareness. When and if he discovered that money could be used generously to express love for himself and others, he would have stumbled upon a universal truth and become "conscious." Realizing that generosity could provide more good feelings and create more wealth than miserliness could, he would have experienced growth in his level of awareness, and he would have realigned with his soul's intent – to grow his self-love.

Let's view this perspective in Billy's case. Suppose he dismissed his father's methods of attaining and keeping wealth. Perhaps something within him realized that his father's methods were counterproductive or hurtful. Perhaps he had suffered enough through his desperate attempts to receive unconditional love from his father that he vowed never to use money as a vehicle for his own acknowledgement of his affection for another. The ways in which Billy could have taken a non-greedy path are endless, but let's examine the results.

As a direct result of Billy's upbringing, he consciously seeks information that proves a better way of living exists. By being conscious or awake, Billy opens himself up to universal truth. He begins observing successful wealthy people and he realizes that wealth comes to those who treat others kindly just as readily as to those who treat others harshly. It appears that you don't have to be a "good" person to attract wealth, but you don't have to be a "bad" one either. If that's the case, why not be a "good" person?

From this viewpoint, Billy is able to open his factory and reward the employees with pleasant working circumstances. Had Billy's viewpoint been married to the idea that only miserly business people made money, he would have not likely been able to succeed financially. However, his belief system supported the idea that he could succeed as a nice guy. As a matter of fact, evidence that made itself obvious to Billy reinforced that not only did kindness allow wealth, it encouraged wealth.

Money is a tool on earth ... simply a tool and nothing else.

Soon Billy prospered. He accumulated wealth and felt great self-love because he recognized that he did so while being a kind person. He felt love for the idea that "kindness gets you farther in life" than being stingy. His dad had been stingy. He was stingy with his money as a way to manage his display of love for others; therefore, he was stingy with his love.

In Billy's personal life, he also realized that his father's paradigm was not aligned with a positive way of thinking. He wanted to try to demonstrate love for others without using or controlling money in his relationships. As such, he grew a natural ability to show love for his family members without needing material demonstrativeness. His children benefited because they grew up with the universal truth that love matters more than money, and that money need not be used as a tool to control the behavior of others. Since they had the privilege of living with universal truth, they did not need to seek it later in life. They had witnessed the model of kindness, affection, and wealth all coexisting harmoniously. As such, money could be earned, accumulated, and spent in productive loving ways, likely without emotional baggage attached to it.

As we said, there are an infinite number of ways that Billy's path could have unfolded based upon his beginnings, so let's examine another possibility.

Billy was so tortured in his youth by his father's incapacity to demonstrate affection in non-material ways, that Billy became distasteful of wealth and material goods. He eschewed all signs of wealth and only felt affection or self-love when he lived with scarcity. The leap he took was to learn to love himself without prosperity in a way that his father had never been able to do. Billy redefined the worth of a person. Perhaps a person's value or lovability was based upon their character and their choices, but too much money corrupted that natural tendency. As a result, this viewpoint allowed money to still be a way to demonstrate love. By not accumulating much, Billy could love himself anyway. However, within this perspective, he would always struggle financially as long as he continued to believe that wealth corrupted a person.

The examples of how money is used as a tool to demonstrate love are endless, but let us give one additional spin on Billy's story. Suppose Billy took to heart that he was not lovable as his father had continuously reinforced. He also became familiar with the pattern that he did not receive material perks when he was not behaving as his father expected him to behave. The idea that he was not lovable combined with the idea that, as his father demonstrated, worthy people are wealthy, led Billy to a self-destructive path of not allowing money. The convoluted unconscious paradigm at work here is that if Billy is unlovable and worthy people are wealthy, then Billy could not be wealthy.

In this case, Billy was using money, or the lack thereof, to demonstrate love. Since he felt unlovable, his belief system would not allow him to become wealthy because wealthy people were worthy.

We could, perhaps, give several more plausible outcomes to Billy's adulthood. Maybe some other scenarios popped into your head as you were reading these examples. If not, try to think of other ways Billy could have played out his life.

It is the partnership between positive, uncorrupted beliefs, and optimism or joy, mixed together with the execution of inspired action that leads to success in any area.

Truth

By understanding the cause and effect of how early exposure to money transactions occur, you are awakening to truth. Whatever your personal circumstances were in your youth are just that – circumstances – not necessarily truth. If you are unhappy with your present financial situation, look at the misbeliefs that you were exposed to as a child, not only from your parents, but also from your religion, your government, or your education.

Right now we are going to tell you the universal truth about money. Every other thing that you have heard or every other thought that you believe is fiction.

Believing that the intellect is a more reliable resource than intuition leads to critical errors.

First, and most importantly, money is a tool on earth for the expression of love. Through money, love can be expressed for oneself, others, humanity, living creatures, the earth, or ideas. An uncomplicated paradigm for life existing within universal truth is that there is prosperity and abundance for all creatures on earth. All ideas have merit and those leading to the expansion of love in any area will prosper. Those which do not will die.

As long as all of humanity embraces and successfully gives and receives love, the natural abundance will be discovered by all.

In an imperfect society where universal truth is not the foremost directive, there is still enough prosperity and abundance for all. Every person is entitled to a happy joyful life filled with the things and experiences that satisfy them. As one person's wealth expands, others' do as well. Prosperity breeds prosperity. Those who are not experiencing wealth are living within the fictitious false ideas that compromised the natural feelings of abundance that they were born with. As long as one false idea became a belief, thus replacing the rightful idea of natural abundance, the ability for that person to experience natural abundance may be compromised.

As long as all of humanity embraces and successfully gives and receives love, the natural abundance will be discovered by all.

At this point, we would like to give you an exercise that will help you to reveal your own belief system in terms of money. This exercise is critical in helping you discover where you are living unconsciously and will awaken you to improved ideas that will help you journey towards riches.

Use the sections/areas on the following pages to reflect upon these thoughts:

What I know about money / What I do not know about money

Take about twenty minutes to fill in the content under each header. Don't think too much ... just write.

Of course, naturally you can "cheat" at this point and continue to read, but then there's really no benefit to you, is there? Please read on after you're finished.

What I know about money	What I do not know about money

Welcome back!

The answer to this question (effectively, "What is money?") was given to you just before you did this exercise. Essentially, that's what was being asked. Do you agree? "What is money?" is the same as "what I know and what I don't know about money"?

The items you listed in your two columns are revealing. Had we asked you to head the columns, **What I know about wealth / What I do not know about wealth,** you probably would have recorded the same exact answers as you actually wrote in response to **What I know about money / What I do not know about money.** True?

If you listed your only answer as "money is a tool for the expression of love on earth," then you fundamentally understand the basic concept that will enable you to propel yourself towards wealth and prosperity. More likely, however, you confused the concept of money with the concept of wealth and prosperity.

Money is a tool on earth for the expression of love; wealth is not. Wealth is perhaps, by one definition, an accumulation of money or material possessions. Wealth also includes a component of other forms of abundance such as an abundance of time, or love, or knowledge. Did you ever hear the expression, a wealth of knowledge?

So highly integrated is today's idea of money with the idea of wealth, that they are often considered synonymous.

Imagine this: A man believes fervently that he will always have everything he wants or needs. He lives in a state of perfect knowingness that all he covets in the material world will be received. With this belief, he doesn't have to set out to earn or accumulate money; he just has to think about what he wants. Suppose he wants tickets to see a play on Broadway … he wins tickets on the radio. He wants a nice beautiful house to live in without a mortgage or rent payments … a friend calls him and asks him to become the caretaker for a nearby park which includes living free of charge in the great house on the acreage. He wants food. His brother opens a restaurant and asks him to be the handyman and offers free meals in lieu of payment.

The foundation for harmony within the money model is not your relationship with others: it's your relationship with yourself.

The possibility sounds implausible, and perhaps it is highly unlikely, but provided this man has the capability of purely believing that he will have everything he wants, it can continue. He must have no fear, no baggage nor misbeliefs that abundance is scarce or money must be earned to live. As a matter of fact, when man first inhabited the earth, this belief was the only belief among all people. They understood that the world, or the universe, would provide all that they ever needed or wanted and, as such, lived in perfect harmonious balance with the earth, plants, and nature.

Since it is possible to live without money and still be wealthy, it is very possible that money is not wealth. Money is a tool on earth, simply a tool and nothing else.

If you set your goal of savings at $10,000 and this is the magic number that will make you feel wealthy, then you will never feel true prosperity before that. If you approach the number and then increase it to $100,000, then you will never feel wealthy until you have reached that number. Is it at all possible to feel wealthy and eliminate your fear about scarcity without focusing on a fixed amount of accumulated money? Yes, it is.

By doing the exercises in the second half of this book, you will do just that. You can set goals, but you will also experience the sensation of feeling prosperous before you hit your personal magic numbers in wealth. The exercises allow you to move from a belief system of scarcity and lack to one of abundance and ease in accumulating wealth. Since it is inevitable that the proper execution of these exercises will lead you to your goals, you will be encouraged to continue by your successes being incrementally realized. This optimistic feeling will work towards changing maligned beliefs about wealth towards positive beliefs. It is the partnership between positive, uncorrupted beliefs, and optimism or joy, mixed together with the execution of inspired action that leads to success in any area.

These exercises will provide the mechanism to change your beliefs, if you let them. That means that you must earnestly cooperate with the exercises. If you don't believe that they can change your life, then do nothing and nothing will change. If, after six months of doing nothing your relationship with money is the same as it is today, then try the exercises at that time and see what happens. Apparently, there is no harm in trying, but there is potential harm in not trying.

Intuition versus Logic

We wish to change the topic and look back at the recent exercise. If we knew that the only inspired or knowledgeable answer with credibility was that money was a vehicle on earth for the expression of love, why would we ask you to spend twenty minutes at the task? The reason is that it takes people an average of twenty minutes absorbed in a task to get themselves out of the way. This means that intuition can become the dominant mechanism in action as opposed to logic. Why is this significant, using intuition instead of logic?

There are two, and only two, reasons that life on earth is imperfect. One is that people have forgotten that the purpose of life is to love, to create, and to learn, in that order; there are no exceptions. The second is that people are enamored with their logic and believe that it is a more reliable source than their intuition. All problems ensue from these two critical errors.

Did you ever take a multiple choice test and get an immediate response to a question, then afterwards logically analyze the choices ad nauseam until you were confused about which answer to choose? The first "hit" was your intuition, and the second reaction was your logic. It was more likely, statistically, that the first answer was correct than any alternate choice. This example simplistically illustrates that if you use your intuition more you will "get more right." Developing or reconnecting with intuition is the surest way to improve your life.

We previously indicated to you that we would give you examples of what life "here" is like. There is no "place" since there is truly no such thing as "space," yet we embrace the reality we create the way those with a physical body embrace their reality. Most people on earth believe in the concepts of time and space. They often believe that life happens randomly and the best defense or offense is to take it as it comes and avoid risk.

Here, in the energy realm, we don't take it as it comes and we don't avoid risk. We create our lives through our thoughts and our beliefs and through cooperative agreement with all that has been created around us. It sounds odd for us to use language such as "all around us" if there is no such thing as space and, likewise, to state action language like "create" or "take it as it comes" if there is no such thing as time. The idea of existing without these two "laws" is so complicated for humans to conceptualize, that we will use the language of time and space to metaphorically illustrate our journey "here." To illustrate a moment of creation in the energy realm, consider this example:

Money is a tool for the expression of love.

I was looking at a spectacular view and I realized that I was weary from standing. To my left was a beautiful sunflower that stood to about half my height. The sunflower immediately recognized my thoughts and moved itself into the shape of a stool and offered itself to me as a place to rest. I sat down upon the sunflower stool and continued to watch the view. This arrangement is known as "cooperative agreement."

All that has been created interacts with all else in mutual advantageous agreement.

As we imagine you realize, we never tell a pointless story. Think about why we relayed this incident to you. It talks about creating our reality and it indicates a practical application of cooperative agreement. How might these concepts be of value to you now?

Money will work cooperatively with you if you allow your beliefs to absorb the ideas about money in this book. Since, in actuality, humans create their reality through their thoughts and beliefs the same way that we do in the energy realm, working cooperatively with money will ensure that you create the reality that you choose rather than create the reality that you are not "wanting."

Begin telling money [and the universe] what you want and it will comply. The laws in which earth life exists have no choice but to obey. If you told yourself that you didn't believe in the law of gravity anymore, guess what? You are still not going to float by the ceiling without first creating a vacuum to isolate this law from its effect on you. Likewise, you cannot change the law that the universe wants to provide you with what you want. If you do not have what you want, you have merely been giving the wrong messages to the universe. The second half of this book will allow you to change that pattern. The steps contained herein allow you to modify what it is that you are telling the universe in order to align the law's intent with your true desires. Overcoming maligned beliefs will greatly allow this transition to occur, and the mystery about how to overcome maligned beliefs is erased when you follow the recommendations in this book and earnestly try to apply its concepts and exercises.

Is it necessary to understand why your muscles biologically respond to your brain's instructions in order to successfully run? No. You will not necessarily become a better, more efficient, or faster runner with this knowledge. If you understand why or how the universe sets out to provide you with what you want [actually with what you believe], will it make it more likely to happen? No. Learn the techniques and let the law work on your behalf, for you, instead of against you.

You Know it All

There is no reason to continue reading this book because you now know everything you really need to know about money. If you would like to learn more about attaining and retaining material wealth, however, then continue.

Using the model that money is a vehicle for the expression of love, let's assume that you know how to love. Your relationships are wonderful, not only with your mate and family, but with your neighbors, coworkers, teammates, and so on. If all this is true, then shouldn't you have no money worries? Since you are experiencing an abundance of reciprocal love, your need to use money as a tool to give or receive love should be harmonious, enough for all, and all happily abundant. The truth is that the foundation for harmony within the money model is not your relationship with others; it's your relationship with yourself. It is not until you unconditionally love yourself that you achieve a natural state of harmony within this model with others.

What's interesting is that all non-harmonious exchanges of money happen because the giver or the receiver has a diminished love of self. To bring this concept into terms that are easier to understand, first let's define a "harmonious exchange." Harmony is balance. When money is exchanged, a balance between giver and taker is present if both parties received an equivalent value in the exchange. If you purchase a carton of eggs for $1.49, it is likely that you felt $1.49 worth of value in giving the store this money. It is likely that the clerk felt justified in taking the $1.49 from you and it's likely that the proprietor of the store felt that $1.49 was a fair amount for the eggs, allowing for the cost of the eggs to be recuperated and a reasonable profit to be realized. The entire exchange was harmonious for all involved.

Now suppose the eggs suddenly cost, due to market conditions, $10.49. The exchange of money is likely to lose balance because one or more parties in the exchange may have an emotional reaction to the price. Perhaps the clerk thinks the price is absurd and concludes that you must be a stupid rich person for paying it. Perhaps the proprietor did not tack on the normal markup because the cost was so great as to be prohibitive to the consumer; therefore, she feels agitated when someone purchases eggs and nothing else. Maybe you get a pinching feeling in your gut as you spend this sum on the eggs.

As you can see, the balance has changed. Emotions have entered into the exchange and money has indeed reflected its role in earth-life as a vehicle for expressing love. If the store owner feels self-love, she may have decided to include her usual profit on the purchase price. Clearly, her attitude that the consumer is getting something for nothing is not evidence of self-love or love of others. If her self-love were whole, her other option would have been to leave the profit off, but feel really good about helping out her customers in this way. This attitude would actually fuel a validation of her lovableness.

Perhaps your self-love was diminished as well when you paid the money. Your thoughts may have been, "What a scam … the chicken people taking advantage of us this way." This attitude in the exchange would have made you feel a degree of powerlessness if you felt you really needed the eggs.

How might your participation in the purchase have been different if your self-esteem were whole? You may have thought, "I'm sure this condition is temporary and I really want the eggs. I feel good about buying them because I feel worthy of the price." Or, you may have opted not to purchase the eggs and felt self-love for exercising good judgment.

Ideally? You would have been at a place in your level of awareness that allowed you to know that there is an abundance of all for everyone on earth. Spending the money would not have created an emotional reaction, but perhaps given you pause to consider that everyone is doing the best that they can within their level of awareness, and the present plight of the chicken farmers may be a way for their group to gain attention or recognition that they were unconsciously wanting. Since thoughts and beliefs create not only your reality, but everyone's reality, the collective beliefs within a region, a group, or an organization amass to carry energy greater than the individuals'.

Changing your perception about the mindless interactions that transpire every day takes time. Let's explore the egg crisis further to see how global the premise that "money is a vehicle for the expression of love" really is. Suppose in this entirely fictitious representation, the chicken farmers of the Northeast were used to receiving a stipend or farm-aid from the federal government. The money was used as the farmers saw fit, but the premise was to allow the farmers to continue to produce while the consumer realized a reasonable price for eggs. Due to governmental cutbacks, this stipend was drastically reduced. The farmers, feeling entitled to the money, became irate and fearful. They felt cheated out of something they believed they deserved forever and they also became fearful that their present way of life was in jeopardy. The fear grew as the farmers began to focus on every penny increase in feed, and they began to congregate to discuss their plight. Now the thought energy and collective belief system began to create, exponentially, more fear and more feelings of being wronged.

Soon, the price of egg cartons doubled. Gas prices soared, increasing distribution costs and the cost of their operations' electricity. Things kept getting worse. A virus eliminated a portion of the egg-laying population. Now the fear grew worse as well.

Most of what went wrong after the governmental supplement decrease was a direct or indirect reaction to the fear and anger on which the farmers collectively focused – creating a greater crisis than the decrease in supplement itself had created. Where does love play into this scenario? The legislators enacting the cuts loved themselves by responding to constituents' desire to see governmental costs decreased. By chiseling the expenditures, they were hoping to gain votes in the next election – which they hoped, in turn, would contribute to their reelection. In many politicians' realities, being elected or reelected is an affirmation of their lovability. In the reality of altruistic politicians who intend to "make their world a better place," being elected validates not only their lovability, but also affirms their love of others since the people allegedly voted for the ideals behind their political campaigns.

In this case, the farmers had loved themselves by accepting the government's financial assistance. By accepting this money, they were indicating that they deserved the aid to compensate for whatever circumstances were deemed beyond their control, and that they were worthy of the money. They expressed love for the idea that supplementing farmers' incomes was the right thing to do, or at least love for themselves by thinking, "If all the other farmers are taking the money, why shouldn't I?"

The farmers also loved themselves by passing on the distress costs to the proprietors, therefore, the consumers. By allowing themselves to receive the same profit margin per carton after the reduction of aid and the increased costs, they were indicating that they were worthy of the same standard of living as they had previously.

The prevalent assumption that many exchanges of money are random and not determined by the beliefs of the parties involved is false.

In what different ways might the farmers have indicated love of self? A farmer may have realized that his egg selling future is limited because of the external changes. He may suddenly intuit that he had always wanted to raise fruit instead of eggs and now would be the perfect time to change. He might passionately believe in himself and begin the process of immediately supplementing his production with the growth of fruit trees or bushes. He may even love the government for enabling him to embrace his dream, upon which he had been resisting acting.

The possibilities of how he could demonstrate love are endless, but this example demonstrates how he showed love for himself by spending [giving] money for fruit production paraphernalia and crops, and remaining confident in himself or the universe that he was capable of thriving without receiving the supplemental income.

You might think twice about what's going on behind the exchange next time you purchase eggs.

Love

Every interaction resulting in the exchange of (or decision not to exchange) money can be viewed in terms of money as a tool for the expression of love.

This knowledge matters for a reason. It can be expanded upon, not only to make sense of where we are with money, but also to be used as a guide for future interactions with money. In order to apply this knowledge to the best of our ability, we must understand more about love.

Make conscious choices once you feel you understand the direction you should take in working towards your goals.

Every human being on earth wants to be appreciated. There is a universal desire to be wanted, valued, liked, and, ultimately, loved. If you think about your interaction with people, regardless of whether or not an exchange of money is involved, the interchange always has a more positive outcome if all parties respect or appreciate one another. If you are rude to a store clerk, the interaction will not have as favorable an outcome as if you are friendly and personable. If you are dismissive of the wait staff, your interaction with them will not be as happy as if you had been respectful.

Appreciation is the beginning of the thing we call "love." It may not be an intense feeling of emotion, but it is the basic ingredient for all love. Learning to appreciate others takes practice and desire. Careful consistent appreciation of others leads to a fundamental form of love called "tolerance." Once again, tolerance may not be a fireworks kind of sentiment, but it provides a foundation or basis for the truer expression of love.

To appreciate others and to be tolerant of others combine to form a natural state of awareness: being free of judgment. Think about what thoughts run through your head when you meet someone, when you read about someone, or when you think about someone. These thoughts can be measured in their ability to create an increase or decrease in your appreciation or tolerance of someone. For example, if you read about a politician's platform, do you assess the merit of the ideas or the merit of the person relaying the ideas? If you disagree with the platform, do you dislike the politician? Or do you feel tolerant of the person but intolerant of his or her ideas?

The next time you hear views that oppose yours, try to value the person with the different opinion.

Is it possible to appreciate a politician whose ideas you disagree with? Is it possible to feel that person has worth as a human even if you do not care for his views on a particular matter? It sounds like such an easy question that would lead you to believe that you would have to be pretty un-evolved if you answered "no," but the truth is humans judge other humans all the time. They judge their views, their speech, their color, their gender, their religious beliefs, their political agendas, their weight, their hairstyles, their clothing, their cars, their parenting, their careers, their choices. The majority of people judge the person behind the ideas. If they feel the ideas are detrimental or without merit, then they judge the person with the ideas as detrimental, or wrong, or bad.

The first step in growing your ability to understand love is to understand tolerance and appreciation. The next time you hear views that oppose yours, try to value the person with the different opinion. There is so much teaching on earth, thankfully, about tolerance as opposed to prejudice, but few reflect upon tolerance as a universal step towards love. After trying out your ability to tolerate others with differing opinions, then work towards appreciating those people with views contrary to yours. Why is this important and what does it have to do with wealth or money? Well, by understanding and practicing consciously expressing your love, you will be better capable of consciously expressing love through the exchange of money. The more you exercise your ability to love, the greater probability there is to become or remain wealthy.

Think about community meetings. You have probably witnessed or read about community meetings where violence ensued. Was the person to throw the first blow tolerant of the person who had a differing opinion? No, most definitely not. Not only was the idea rejected, but the person proclaiming the idea was rejected as well.

In a civil, evolved society, people are at a minimum tolerant of each other's opinions. That tolerance enables the most basic element of love to be displayed, resulting in a better outcome than in a state where tolerance is not demonstrated.

How does the exchange of money play out in this scenario? Money can be used to express love or a lack thereof. If a person acts out of hatred, he may choose to spend money to damage the idea or the person behind the idea. An example is a "smear" campaign during an election race. If a person acts out of love, he may instead choose to spend money by supporting a candidate with like views, or to increase awareness about his ideas.

Every time money is exchanged, an expression of love is involved.

We're going to give you three hypothetical situations. See if you can figure out what's going on in them with regard to money as an expression of love.

- a bible student studying The Book pays his tuition bill
- a woman pays $300 to a salon to have her hair colored and styled
- a child donates one dollar to the family whose child is sick

If you spend more than a few cursory moments examining each one, you'll see that expressions of love [or a lack thereof] are being made through the exchange of money. In these examples, love of ideas, love of self, and love of others are being demonstrated.

Let's look at a few more examples:

- a terrorist buys a gun
- a police department purchases guns
- a hunter purchases a gun

Slightly different examples of how the exchange of money is expressing love or the lack thereof. Take the time to think about each for a few minutes in terms of love. What is the purchaser showing love for? What is the purchaser showing hatred for?

Here's one more set of examples. Again see if you can determine how love [or the lack thereof] for self, others, ideas, living things, inanimate objects, the planet, or ideas is being expressed.

- a man spends $2000 to attend a Global Warming fund raiser
- a woman donates $25 to the artists painting a mural in the cancer ward's waiting room
- a person spends $100 to receive CPR training

While the possibilities for examples are endless, the concept is not. Every exchange of money is an expression of love.

Now that you understand this message, how can the concept help you improve your relationship with money? Understand that self-love is the weightiest of all influences in the exchange or accumulation of money.

Self-Love

What you now know about money: Money is a vehicle on earth for the expression of love – love of self, love of others, love of living things, love of inanimate objects, love of earth, and love of ideas, with the weightiest influence during any exchange being self-love.

The obvious next step in improving your relationship with the exchange of money towards growing wealth is to check your self-love. What is your opinion of yourself? What is your belief about yourself? What influences your self-confidence? During what situations do you feel invincible and powerful? When do you feel powerless?

This line of questioning is a platform for a book in itself, but for now, please take the time to review the answers to the questions. Try to link your ideas of yourself to your exchanges of money with others. Let us give you some examples of this process so that you may complete the exercise independently and effectively.

Exchange (or lack of exchange) of Money	Possible Self-love Influences in Exchange
Cut back on Starbucks coffee	1. Sense diminished self-worth because I cannot afford what I enjoy 2. Build confidence by demonstrating discipline 3. Love myself enough to know cutback is temporary
Buy $80 perfume (cologne) for self	1. Reinforce my belief that I make unwise decisions 2. I deserve it
Get laid off at work	1. I cannot hold a job (low self-confidence) 2. I think I might be able to land on my feet (moderate confidence) 3. What a great opportunity to start my own business (high self-confidence)

It is worth examining these examples somewhat to assist you in determining how self-love issues affect the exchange of money.

If you are feeling a lack of abundance and then reduce your frequency of purchasing Starbucks coffee, how might your self-love be affecting the decision to reduce the exchange of money? (Remember, the goal here is to determine the root of the exchange, not the reason for the lack of abundance. The roots of each exchange, over time, accumulate to reflect your beliefs about yourself and abundance.) Do you feel worthy of enjoying Starbucks anytime you choose? Do you feel inadequate as an earner, causing you to reinforce your inadequate feelings by giving up something you enjoy? Do you feel enormous confidence in your earning ability and enjoy the challenge of driving through this temporary period, knowing that you will succeed? Do you feel smart in cutting back during the temporary period of low cash flow?

Let's look at the perfume [cologne] purchase. Do you feel guilty (diminished self-worth) after frivolous purchases? Do you love treating yourself to the things that bring you pleasure, knowing that you can have anything you want, always? Are you feeling unhappy and use the pick-me-up purchase to elevate your mood, thus your feelings of optimism and self-worth?

It takes a great deal of reflection to understand what self-love factors may affect your transactions.

Getting laid off is far more complicated because more thought energy and beliefs went into the cutoff of the exchange of money between you and your employer. In every exchange, all parties involved in the exchange have self-love influences affecting it, but they are less apparent during a money exchange involving a purchase. When you purchase a cup of Starbucks coffee, the exchange is relatively insignificant, so determining the other factors of love influencing the transaction (the self-love of the Starbucks employee, the love within and regarding the organization, etc.) is unimportant.

When a person is released from a position, particularly when a layoff is due to cost factors rather than poor employee performance, the complexity of love issues influencing the withdrawal of future payments is immense. It takes a great deal of reflection to understand what self-love factors may have been at work. Let's examine some possibilities.

You had wanted to start your own business for a long time, but fear had prevented you from taking the risk. The layoff may have occurred in response to your belief that you would succeed at your new business, thus eliminating the fear that quitting your job was creating. Your layoff may be a result of extreme self-doubt – doubt in your ability to consistently create abundance. Perhaps you wanted to interview for another company, but hesitated because of a lack of confidence.

An important aspect in the exchange of money is how you view the exchange afterwards. Every exchange provided an opportunity to grow your self-love or for your self-love to be diminished. Obviously, you will not think in these terms for every single transaction that you participate in, but it is a valuable exercise to review most transactions in these terms for a brief period, and then to continue to review all large transactions in these terms afterwards.

You purchase perfume. Afterwards, you have two choices. You can feel glad about the purchase or you can feel unhappy about the purchase. If you feel you overspent or the purchase was frivolous, you can feel diminished self-love or you can restore your self-love by returning the item. If you feel happy about your purchase, your self-love does not require additional examination.

This review may seem like abundance is dependent upon self-love. It often is. To be happy about the purchase of the perfume, you must love yourself enough to feel worthy of it, and you must feel a great enough sense of self-love that your abundance is present and will continue to be present. In other words, you love yourself enough to allow abundance to be a continuing part of your journey.

Self-love is not the only factor influencing the exchange of money in your life, but it is the fundamental factor. Most people have an underlying belief about what they are worth in terms of material possessions and comforts, and their level of abundance will reflect that belief. The reason you are determining your self-love influence in monetary transactions is to help you determine your overall self-love profile. When you see a pattern in your decisions to purchase or not, or you recognize a pattern in how outside influences affect the quantity of money you receive, you can understand your self-love profile.

Most people have an underlying belief about what they are worth, and their level of abundance will reflect that belief.

We would like to add a comment that is critical at this point. There is a prevalent assumption that many exchanges of money are random and not determined by the beliefs of the parties involved. This assumption is false.

To illustrate, whether the stocks you purchase will appreciate or decline in value is determined by the same factors that affect every exchange of money in which you participate. Further, the parties involved are endless. The first degree of influence is you and the financial organization's representative (in a commission structured transaction). The second level of influence may be the department head or your spouse. The third level of influence may be the CEO of the financial organization or your economics teacher. All parties that influenced the transaction have the potential to affect the outcome. If your economics teacher taught you information that allowed you to believe you are empowered in the stock market and can always succeed financially, the influence is obviously positive. However, if the teacher allowed you to believe that the overall successfulness of a stock portfolio was based upon governmental economic decisions, then you are likely to believe that you are powerless in influencing the outcome.

Now it may sound like you have no power in a transaction, but let us prove to you how great your power really is. Your self-love (reflected in your beliefs) determined what economics teacher you would get and how you would integrate the information that you were presented with. A possibility is that you consciously or unconsciously sensed your power in affecting the outcome of future stock purchases. (In other words, your high self-love allowed you to feel powerful in creating wealth.) The universe is likely to match your belief system with the teacher who is most likely to reinforce your beliefs. The magnetic properties of the law of attraction may then have presented you with a teacher who introduced you to the vast possibilities available in the stock market, thus igniting your passion for this pursuit.

On the other hand, you may have gotten a teacher who emphatically reinforced the powerlessness in predicting stock portfolio outcomes. With your extremely high self-love or feeling of power, however, you may integrate the information as a challenge to prove that you are capable beyond your teacher's inability to believe that anyone has power.

Through this example, you can see how the law of attraction works. You can see that the possibility exists that your teacher propelled you towards your interest in pursuing stock investing through positive commentary about the possibilities or through negative commentary about the possibilities for attaining wealth through this method. The reason that different possibilities [teachers] may be magnetized towards you is because of the belief system of the other party and the thought energy that he is putting forth. For example, if he highly believed that it's difficult to gain wealth through stock investment, he may have magnetized you in as a student for the opportunity to hear a different perspective about the possibilities. You may awaken him to a new view through your thoughts, research, or success in investing.

The point is that you and your teacher each had "charged" thoughts about this topic. The more highly your thoughts are charged, the more readily the law of attraction works to create the match. Back to the original example, if you had extremely low self-love or confidence and then attracted in the teacher with negative views towards the possibility of attaining wealth through stock investing, the teacher's views would strengthen your view. If you were then to invest, you would likely have unfavorable results to the degree that your thoughts were "charged."

Of course, we are oversimplifying these examples to help you understand the role of self-love and thought-energy. Take the necessary steps to feel good about yourself and know that you are entitled to a wonderful reality on earth with all the joys and experiences that you desire.

What Do You Want?

Let's begin the practical section of this book. What follows is the actions that, when consistently taken, will lead to the improvement of your financial situation.

If you have a partner with whom you share your financial reality, it is most beneficial for the two of you to perform these exercises together. The combined results of effective focus may prove to be far more satisfying, meaning "beneficial," than working alone may be.

TASK ONE

Define your needs, not your wants – your needs. Add up your monthly expenses, add in an estimated figure for your tax liability (based on your financial history or input from your tax professional), and multiply the figure by twelve to determine your annual "needs" income. For example:

Monthly Expense	Amount
Mortgage	$1500
Real estate taxes	500
Phone services	235
Internet / Cable	100
Food	350
Fuel - Home	200
Fuel – Auto(s)	200
Electric	160
Water	30
Car payment	425

Lawn service (Is this really a need?)	N/A
Clothing (what's needed, not wanted)	100
Insurance	250
Other (gifts, charity, etc.)	200
TOTAL	$4250

Now for estimating taxes and calculating the amount as an annual figure:

$4250 + 25%[1] [$1063] for taxes = $5313
$5313 x 12 months = $63,756 Annual Income

Complete your list:

Monthly Expense	Amount
Mortgage or Rent	$
Food	
Phone services	
Internet / Cable	
Electric	
Fuel – Home	
Fuel – Auto(s)	
Water	
Car payment	
Clothing	
Insurance	
Other (gifts, charity, etc.)	

1 The estimated percentage of your individual tax liability (Federal and State) can be determined by your previous tax return history or with input from your financial professional.

TOTAL	$

Calculation for approximation of taxes:

$__________ + __________% x 12 mos = $__________

TOTAL + [est. tax bracket percentage] x 12 mos = Annual $ Need

There you have it. What you need. Not what you want … what you need. This amount is hardly enough to keep you comfortable, since the goal is always to keep ahead of rising costs plus allow for a reasonable amount of pleasure expenses, yes? What do you think? What is your financial goal? Have you ever defined it? Do you want to be comfortable? Secure? Filthy rich?

Now is the time to think it over. What do you want? Fifty percent more than you currently earn? One hundred percent? One thousand percent? No mortgage? No debt? More play money? More money to help others? A million dollars? So much to decide … take your time.

Well ... the good news is that whatever you decide now you can change later. You can be modest now and increase your desires as you begin to witness the universe providing what it is that you want. Or you can, perhaps, realize later that all the money you desire now is burdensome and you really want far less. Sounds possible, doesn't it?

All of these questions require that you do some serious thinking about money and wealth, and the place or value that they have in your life. Take a little time to determine what you believe about wealth because it will help to determine exactly how much you accumulate. If you are poverty conscious, how can you eliminate this view in your own life or for your own accumulation of wealth? If you believe that rich people are greedy, can you yourself be wealthy without being greedy? As you learned from **THE ANSWERS**, you begin to alter a non-productive association with wealth, health, or relationships by determining where your limiting beliefs lie. From this new perspective, you create your new healthy paradigm in any of these areas.

For the purposes of this book, let's continue with the understanding that you have wrestled with your beliefs and determined that they now reflect, with comfort, the level of wealth you desire.

Create a new list of how much you want. You can build upon the old list, create an entirely new one, or change the figures in the amounts column – you decide. You may even work from the bottom line – doubling or tripling or "hundred-timesing" the amount you want. The following is an imaginary example of your new financial goal:

Monthly Expense	**Amount**
Mortgage	$1500
Real estate taxes	500
Phone services	235
Internet / Cable	100
Food	450
Fuel – Home	200
Fuel – Auto(s)	200
Electric	250
Water	30
Car payment	600
Lawn service	90
Clothing (what's *wanted*, not *needed*)	400
Insurance	350
Take out /eat out	400
Vacations	1000
Toys or recreation	200
Books, music, movies	150
Savings / Investment	2000
Other (gifts, charity, etc.)	400
Contingencies fund	500
TOTAL	$9555

Remember to add in the amount needed for tax payments and multiply by twelve for your new annual "want" amount.

$9555 + 25% for taxes [$2389] x 12 months = $143,328

Create your want list:

Monthly Expense	Amount
Mortgage or Rent	$
Phone services	
Internet / Cable	
Food	
Fuel – Home	
Fuel – Auto(s)	
Electric	
Water	
Car payment	
Clothing (what's *wanted*, not *needed*)	
Insurance	
Take out /eat out	
Vacations	
Toys or recreation	
Books, music, movies	
Savings / Investment	
Other (gifts, charity, etc.)	
Contingencies fund	
TOTAL	$

Calculation for approximation of taxes:

$___________ + __________% x 12 mos = $___________

TOTAL + [est. tax bracket percentage] x 12 mos = Annual $ Want

Suppose you were already there. What would you want next? Will there ever be a goal that is completely satisfying, or will you continue to press towards achieving new ones? Exactly. You will keep pressing. The human soul wants to set new goals, wants to achieve new aspirations. The point? Don't concern yourself with whether or not you set your want-list too low. As you achieve new levels, you will naturally venture towards more challenging objectives.

What you learned in **THE ANSWERS** is that your want list is a living document – it changes when you change or when you want to change. You can alter any part at any time to reflect your evolving wants. No one needs to know what is on your list unless you feel the desire to share it. There is no judgment from others, only judgment from yourself. As such – decide not to judge the content of your want list from a negative perspective. You are not required to demonstrate a certain amount of charitable contribution to be worthy of wealth. You are not required to justify your desire for a weekly massage or a Mercedes. You do not have to forego the pleasure of a vacation to pay for school. The truth is that you can have it all as long as you believe you can have it all and you want it.

Your money list is your declaration to the universe. Now

the universe knows what you want. Until now, you would hardly believe how you've been messing with the universe. You had a stroke of financial good luck and all of sudden you started to worry, "Will this continue?" Or you thought, on some level, "Uh oh … things are going really well. I wonder when it's all gonna fall apart." Picture the universe's confusion. "She said she wanted this, and now, look! She seems like she doesn't really want it after all – pull back, guys. Get this money out of here – QUICK! It's causing her pain not pleasure."

Then you settled down and started telling the universe again that you want wealth – monetary wealth. As you send out mixed signals upon receipt of the wealth – the universe will pull back, even reverse recent fortunes.

Your money list is your declaration to the universe.

So, once more, be clear about what you want. Do not vacillate because you just cause the universe's head to spin. (That's a metaphor. The universe doesn't really have a head that spins. However, if you visualize this metaphor, you can recognize the humor and futility in sending mixed messages.)

Recognize, deep within you, that you are entitled to whatever you want. There are no universe rules or limits; there are only man-made rules and limits. Don't subscribe to them. They weren't written for you.

Reflection

Before we get to the next exercise, we want to remind you of the universe's definition of greed. As laid forth in **THE ANSWERS**, greed is when you accumulate more than you can value or appreciate. When ownership becomes burdensome, then ownership has become greedy. For example, many people are comfortable owning $100,000 in savings, but when that figure reaches $500,000 they become uncomfortable. They may fear embezzlement or fraud. They may fear losing control over such a large fund. When the figure approaches $5 million, people who are most comfortable at a savings level of $100,000 become overwhelmed. They become paranoid about people no longer wanting relationships with them for who they are, but rather for what they have. Holding onto the money becomes a great source of fear and the supposed freedom that was gained by the wealth is excised.

When a person no longer finds pleasure in ownership, the ownership is greed. Be mindful of the distinction. If you are happy and revel in the pleasure of your ownership of $5 million, you are not being greedy. You are wanting and appreciating all that you have and the universe will happily comply with your wants by letting you keep it.

You'd be surprised (or perhaps not surprised at all) by the number of souls embroiled in money battles because the universe provided an opportunity for them to create that which they focused on – fear of losing control. The unending battle validates the initial fears, the belief that "others are out to get what is mine."

At this point, understanding what money is will help you engage in the exercises put forth. This moment in your life is pivotal; it is the moment when you choose your own abundance. You choose to let go of misbeliefs and engage in the life-fulfilling process of allowing abundance.

There are no universe rules or limits; there are only man-made rules and limits. Don't subscribe to them. They weren't written for you.

For every successful change that occurs at the level of the mind, the occurrence must be transferred to the physical in order for the change to occur in reality. There are two necessary actions for you to take for this success to happen. First, reflect upon what you want every day, three times a day. Abstractly, you have been doing this your entire life and the results have brought you exactly what has presently manifested in your reality. You, perhaps, did not actively recognize the messages that you were putting forth every day – but they exist and now you want to "correctly align" the messages with that which you know you want.

For example, you were profoundly influenced by others' ideas of money throughout your life. Try to determine what some of the influences on your beliefs were. Is money hard to come by? Is it hard to hold? Is there never enough? Do you need to postpone pleasure for the pain of responsibilities? Do you need to sacrifice what you want for your children?

Your own thoughts have actively *instructed* the universe about what you believe and the universe has complied by *providing* that which you believe. That's what the universe does; it complies with your beliefs. Reflecting now, three times a day, upon the improved belief system that you are adopting will help the beliefs take root and flourish, and will allow the universe to begin providing within that belief system.

What does "reflect" mean? How do you reflect upon your list? Well, there are limitless ways. Some people like to meditate, others to pray. Some prefer visualizing, while others prefer reading. Others, still, prefer an auditory method of reflecting. What works best for you? The method is not relevant. Whichever method you use, the important factor is that you are feeling good while doing it. No worrying allowed. No doubt admitted. No fear permitted! Just feel good about the possibility of this want list coming true. You can do it. And the universe will provide the items on the list for you. Believe in it and feel good while reflecting upon it.

Action

The second action that will successfully move the "ideas" and beliefs into creating reality is action itself. Take action.

Take inspired action. Be mindful of the thought energy you put forth into the universe when you take action, but take action. Doing nothing differently will get you exactly where you are right now and you are reading this workbook because you are not thrilled with exactly where you are right now.

Action has some misbeliefs of its own attached to its meaning. For some reason, it connotes the idea that any action is good action. That is false, completely false and counterproductive. If you spend great amounts of energy taking action that is fruitless or not properly charged to attract in success, then you will be spinning your wheels endlessly, getting nowhere fast.

We're going to begin by learning how to take action. Which actions are worthy? Which are fruitless? How can you decide what actions to take for the maximum impact?

Put aside some time now to brainstorm. Ideally, begin with a *minimum* of twenty minutes. The first exercise is to determine possible ways in which you can achieve the financial goals on your list. If you have a career in which you believe you can achieve these goals, then skip this next section.

[If continuing with current career, go to PAGE 89*]

What possible ways can you attract in the income or wealth that you want? Where do your passions lie? What is your educational background? Where is your experience centered? As you consider these ideas, focus heavily on *what you want.* Do you want to continue in sales if that is your profession? Do you want to use your nursing degree to attain wealth? Is there something else that you think you may want to try for earning money?

Where do your passions lie?

Consider sources of revenue other than just earned income. Do you see yourself succeeding in investing in the stock market? Real estate? Multi-level marketing? What passive forms of income can you consider?

Brainstorm the answers to these questions. Only you know where your passions lie. The best path to earning income or attracting in wealth is to focus on what you enjoy doing. What do you love? Consider strongly ways to earn or attract wealth through what brings you pleasure.

Allow yourself at least twenty minutes to jot down your ideas. Leave no thought unrecorded. This list is for your personal benefit. Do not censor yourself in content or ideas. Keep going as long as the ideas are flowing regardless of how long it takes; the more the better.

Possible Ways I Can Attract in Income or Wealth

Hopefully, you have had some realizations about yourself through this exercise. Perhaps you realized that you really don't have a clue what you want. Maybe you have realized that you want something that you believe is unattainable. Maybe you now understand that your present form of income is your passion.

Where are your limiting beliefs? Do you believe that you can't become a lawyer because you are fifty? There's no money to be made as an actor? You don't have savings so you can't possibly invest in real estate?

Overpower your limiting beliefs. How many stories have you heard of someone changing her entire life at age forty and attaining all she dreamed afterwards? What has happened in your life so far is not an indication of what will unfold in the future unless you *believe* it is an indication of what will happen in the future. Now is the moment to redefine what you believe.

Overpower your limiting beliefs.

Your next exercise is to determine your intended course. In order to achieve your financial goals, write down clearly what you want to manifest. Do you need to attend school? Do you need to do some research about your new course [of action]? Are there local seminars that can educate you about investing or financial planning? How can you attain the support you need to succeed in this pursuit?

To illustrate this exercise, let's use an example that you are a thirty-five year old man with two small children. You are considered the primary bread winner and work at a job you despise approximately 45 hours per week. You have always wanted to be an attorney, but think it's too late.

How can you manifest that which you want at this point in your life? Will it be easy?

LONG TERM ACTIONS – LIST ONE

[for individuals selecting a new career path]

Make a list of ten doable tasks that will put you closer towards your goals. For example:

1. I will discuss my passion with my spouse and ask for her support.
2. I will find successful attorneys with whom I will discuss this career path so I have a stronger idea of the rewards and pitfalls.
3. I will create a plan with my wife that allows my family to support this pursuit.
4. I will talk to Human Resources to determine what tuition reimbursement program they have available.
5. I will research area or online law school alternatives.
6. I will determine what financial steps I need to take to continue.
7. I will discuss with my boss cutting my work hours to 40 per week while I attend school.
8. I will research entrance requirements and determine if I qualify or what I need to do to qualify.
9. I will select a school.

10. I will create a timeline for applying, qualifying, and beginning.

Use your imagination in creating your first **Long Term Actions List**. For added support, consider allowing someone you respect to help you create this list; after all, your passion is likely to expand as you share your ideas with another. In addition, the unconditional support of another person will act like an exercise program undertaken with a partner – you are more likely to get your butt to the gym when someone is counting on you or aware of your goals than when you commit alone. A partner in focusing on your goals is not necessary, however. Only you can decide whether or not your success possibilities are increased with the involvement of another. Bear in mind that you want to stack the odds in your favor. Do whatever you can think of to create an environment for success.

Ten Tasks That Will Bring Me Closer to My Goals

1. ______________________________

2. ______________________________

3. ______________________________

4. ______________________________

5. ______________________________

6. ______________________________

7. ______________________________

8. ______________________________

9. ______________________________

10. ______________________________

Please join the other readers now with the continuation of this program. Naturally, your first **Long Term Actions List** is complete – the scope of the content is merely different than that for people who are maintaining their current career pursuit.

*[**For readers maintaining present career path, continue reading at this point from page 82]**

LONG TERM ACTIONS – LIST ONE

[for individuals maintaining their present career path]

By now you have a strong idea of what you want to pursue. What actions must you take to achieve your goals? What actions excite you? Consider actions that drive you forward in your present field as well as actions that supplement your current path or move you towards another field. The idea is to keep passion as your motivator. Yes, we must all do certain things that aren't that exciting, but allow your passion to fuel the overall course.

You will create a list of ten actionable items that will bring you closer to your goals. For example:

1. I will brainstorm ways to enhance my present position at work.
2. I will discuss my thoughts, ambitions, and career path with my boss.
3. I will create an action plan with my boss to achieve my goals.
4. I will approach several people who may be interested in real estate investing about beginning a success buddy system.
5. I will research local seminars about real estate investing.
6. I will attend two seminars to educate myself about investing.
7. I will attend networking events that allow me to meet people involved in the real estate fields.
8. I will research steps towards strengthening my credit score.
9. I will take one step towards strengthening my credit score.
10. I will create a timeline for achieving my new career path at work.

Before we continue, we would like to discuss with you support in your pursuit of your goals. If you have a business partner and your actions, rewards, and obstacles are tied into your partner's, it is best for you to undertake this program with him or her. Not only will you both benefit from having common goals, you will also benefit from working together on a clearly defined path towards achieving those goals. Most importantly, provided you are harmonious with one another, your energies will combine to attract in greater success than either can achieve with his or her individual energy. Support is not limited to a business partner. Consider bringing your spouse or mate into your achievement program. You can work together on individual goals, gaining energy, enthusiasm, and commitment from each other. Select your partner carefully. Assure yourself that this individual supports you unconditionally and that your relationship is one that will allow you to grow in your enthusiasm.

Attaining financial wealth requires commitment

Two enthusiastic, mutually supportive energies have an exponential effect on the universe. These energies do not combine to create a double force; they combine to create a tenfold force. These numbers are metaphoric, of course, but understand that the power of two like-energies can affect the universe more than each can individually in separate pursuits.

A partner can also assist you in staying committed. Changing your life is not easy; it is simpler to maintain familiar patterns of thought and behavior. Doing nothing is much easier than doing something that requires commitment. This program towards attaining financial wealth requires commitment.

Create your **LONG TERM ACTIONS LIST**:

Long Term Actions List[2]

1.	
2.	
3.	
4.	
5.	
6.	
7.	
8.	
9.	
10.	

2 For downloadable forms, please visit www.theanswersunlimited.com/MoneyWisdom.html

After each line item, write in a date by which you intend to complete the item. Be reasonable. Be cautious. Be bold. Be strong. Be outlandish. Be conservative. How can you be all these things? Simply choose dates that push you but are doable.

Easy enough?

When first you decide on these dates, you may be inclined to make the task inordinately easy by selecting dates that are easily attainable. Your goal is to move forward in meeting your desires. Set a pace at which you are comfortable. If that means choosing dates that in your mind are easy, then, by all means, do so. The commitment necessary to achieve a new pattern of attraction and actions will be greater if you believe that you can succeed. If, on the other hand, that means choosing rigorous and extraordinarily challenging dates, only you can decide if this method will incite you or burn you out. Be realistic within your own knowledge of yourself. Respect who you are and respect what you believe you are capable of achieving. Meeting the dates is significant, however. If you cannot decide between a sooner or later date, and your hesitation is caused by doubt about the possibility of achieving the sooner date, please choose the later date.

For the purpose of this program, it is better to give yourself the option of accomplishing the tasks before "deadline" than missing the target.

Let's continue with our imaginary list. Assume the creation date is July 12th.

Long Term Actions List	Date
1. I will brainstorm ways to enhance my present position at work.	07.15
2. I will discuss my thoughts, ambitions, and career path with my boss.	07.24
3. I will create an action plan with my boss to achieve my goals.	08.04
4. I will approach some people who may be interested in real estate investing about beginning a success buddy system.	08.06
5. I will research local seminars about real estate investing.	07.22
6. I will attend two seminars to educate myself about investing.	09.15
7. I will attend networking events that allow me to meet people involved in the real estate field.	09.15
8. I will research steps towards strengthening my credit score.	07.20
9. I will take one step towards strengthening my credit score.	08.10
10. I will create a timeline for achieving my new career path at work.	08.15

As you can see, the dates in this example give ample time for contingencies such as seminars not being offered at close dates. The list also gives a reasonable amount of time to achieve goals that may prove beyond your complete control, such as your boss finding time to meet with you. Had the selected date been July 15th, for example, the meeting may not have been able to occur due to scheduling conflicts.

Try to review the list carefully for opportunities to accommodate external factors. Item number one is within your control. Few outside factors can affect your ability to achieve this solo task.

Suppose you became unusually busy at work and at play between the creation date and July 15th which prevented you from accomplishing your list. What happens now?

To be truthful … a lot happens now. Your enthusiasm and commitment are most naturally at its highest point at the inception of any new program. The compromise of this natural enthusiasm before the first expected completion date needs evaluation.

Why did you miss the date? Frankly, we will tell you it is because you are not yet ready to commit to life-changing improvements that will bring into your life what you suppose you want. Does this statement sound harsh to you? Well, it's meant to. If you cannot meet the first, completely independent deadline, you are likely to miss many ensuing deadlines.

Think about what may be compromising your commitment. Are you sure about what you want? Do you believe that the items on your financial goal list are possibilities? Do you understand the difference between a wish and a possibility? Do you want to change? Or are there certain rewards for remaining where you are? Maybe your level of achievement is satisfying to you because not demonstrating more takes the pressure of expectations off you. Not only will you continue achieving at the level others expect of you, but also at the level you expect of yourself. Perhaps you are just not ready to declare to the universe that this goal list is what you really want.

It's silly to continue if you have doubt as to your definitive answers in these areas. You will set yourself up for frustration or disappointment if you are not willing or ready to commit at this time.

Perhaps you're thinking, "Well, I had a chance to go sailing with a friend and work got really busy with everyone taking vacation. It's not my fault that I missed the deadline … I know I'll make it next week."

This is sideways thinking. It allows you to sidestep the obvious and avoid facing the truth. You could have found the time to brainstorm. What are we talking about? Twenty minutes or so? Maybe you could have brought a tape recorder with you on the way to work and brainstormed on the train. Perhaps you could have missed twenty minutes of the game to create the list. There are and there were ways to achieve this deadline. Inaction is indicative of a lack of readiness and only you can determine why.

Please try to solve this issue within yourself before you continue.

Now for those of you who easily met the first few deadlines then suddenly realized that you would not be able to attend two seminars by the fifteenth of September. Why? There simply weren't two offered which you could attend within the timeframe.

This opportunity gives you a chance to realize the importance of the wording in your **Long Term Actions List**. When you are dependent upon circumstances such as date availability or the actions of others, carefully word the item to assure its do-ability. Perhaps better wording would have been, "I will register for the first two real estate investment seminars that I am able to attend." Your commitment is evident in your ability to achieve the line items that are independent of external factors and this commitment will support you in the actual attendance of these events.

Without going into too much detail about what constitutes good wording, remember the goals and keep the goals in your mind as you create your list:

- You want to achieve your financial goals as you outlined them.
- You want to begin and remain enthusiastic about this program because, ultimately, enthusiasm is a vital component for success.
- You want to stay the course. You don't want your tasks or deadlines to be so intimidating that you find any excuse possible to fail or quit.
- You want to give yourself the opportunity to replace ineffective patterns with effective alternatives. As positive replacement behaviors are practiced, you will begin to create new, productive habits.

While we realize that it's almost impossible to make your list ironclad and completely impermeable to external circumstance, do your best to word your tasks with a balance of attainability, challenge, and imperviousness to external factors "beyond your control."

The Universe is Listening

Anyone can make a list. What's the big deal? Why bother? How can this list change your life? Knowing why you are doing something is sometimes as important as knowing how to do it. Basically, the universe wants to provide you with what you want. As a matter of fact, it really doesn't care what you want – it is destined to provide it. Most people get far off the track of achieving that which they believe they want because they haven't told the universe what it is. If you want ten million dollars, but you believe that ownership of this sum is amoral, will be burdensome, or will attract negative people into your life, the universe doesn't determine the inconsistency between these thoughts – wanting or not wanting the money – it simply provided the wants that you believe – not the wants that you think.

> **The universe wants to provide you with what you want.**

The universe understands the difference in energy between the "want" in the mind [thinking] and the "want" which comes from the soul [believing]. Wanting in the mind alone, unsupported by the belief that the desire is possible, cannot make the universe respond and comply. Happy thoughts are just that, happy thoughts. If happy thoughts are coupled with the belief that those happy ideas can come true, they do come true.

Your list is reinforcing to the universe a clear idea of what you want. By reviewing the list and acting in accordance with the actionable items, you are repeatedly telling the universe what you want. The actionable item is not a passing whim; your thoughts, energy, time, commitment, enthusiasm, and beliefs are supporting the want. Check that this statement is true periodically. Are your thoughts, energy, time, commitment, enthusiasm, and beliefs supporting the want?

Your **Long Term Actions List** will drive you towards staying on task in reinforcing your communication with the universe. Because of the significance of the list, meeting the deadlines is important. Our brilliant universe understands that procrastination and missing deadlines is a subtle or subconscious indicator that "you really don't want this so much."

Tell the universe that you do want this. Meet the deadlines. One missed deadline is reasonable. It happens on occasion. Two missed deadlines is understandable, but when you start missing deadlines a third, fourth, or fifth time, you are instructing the universe that you really don't care very much about meeting these goals.

Missing deadlines frequently becomes a habit. The urgency in committing to the dates wanes. You start to realize that you can miss the dates and no immediate negative result appears. What you may fail to recognize, however, is that no positive results are occurring either. Tomorrow is another day. Sure. Commit tomorrow instead of today if you choose, but inadvertently, that is what you have been doing prior to reading this workbook.

Commit to changing your life. Meet the deadlines. If in all

earnestness you've tried and failed, then seriously rework the wording or expectations of your **Long Term Actions List**. Make the tasks achievable.

Meeting deadlines becomes a habit. It is your habits that we are aiming to change. Your new habit will be one in which you consistently and regularly tell the universe what you want.

Is this the only reason for the **Long Term Actions List**? No. Many changes will come to you through unexpected means. In other words, you may have your sights on the goal, but the pathway to the goal may unfold in surprising ways. Often, as you begin to effectively declare what it is you want to the universe, these changes occur through seemingly effortless or passive means. However, action aids in allowing changes to take place more frequently and more readily. Can you declare that you want to be an actor and expect that result without attending auditions, preparing yourself, receiving education or training, or at a minimum, telling others your desire? The result is not likely. It is not entirely impossible, but it is far more likely if you throw your action and energy behind your desire. If you act like you want to become an actor, you will improve the possibility of the outcome.

> **Meeting deadlines becomes a habit. Not meeting deadlines also becomes a habit.**

Cause and consequence has credence. You can help cause the

result you want, the consequence, by taking action. Action should be inspired action. What this means is that the effort you expend should feel fruitful to you. It should fill you with a sense that it's possible to cause the result you want. If you act for the sake of taking action with no enthusiasm or belief that it will aid in your path, then you may as well stay passive because you're wasting your time. It's actually worse than wasting your time – you are creating an environment in which your desire is *less* likely to occur.

Cumulative actions which, over time, are showing no positive results or movement towards the goal will likely diminish your belief in the possibility that the goal is achievable. As you continue to take unenthusiastic actions, the resultant non-success in achievement will further erode your belief in the possibility.

Does this fact mean that you shouldn't do anything that you don't feel like doing? No. The human soul understands that there is a certain amount of activity that must take place in order to achieve larger goals. For example, if you want to become an accountant, is it necessary to love every professor, course, topic, or exam in order to be successful? No, of course not. Your soul will know indirectly or subconsciously that certain tasks are a necessary part of the path.

What you do want to avoid is feeling unenthusiastic about many necessary tasks or a majority of them. If this occurs, think about why. Do you really want to become an accountant? Are you following the course of study to fulfill someone else's desire? Or, perhaps you thought the subject would be appealing to you, but as you study you realize that you have no passion for it.

Also, realize that repeat, dull activities which are necessary to bring you closer to your goal really do not belong on your **Long Term Actions List**. Your list was generated from your enthusiastic brainstorming and, therefore, should primarily contain items that you are enthusiastic about.

Be reasonable and be kind to yourself. If you are starting a retail business, even if you don't want to, you may have to clean your own bathrooms for a while. The task of cleaning a bathroom can be undertaken with two different approaches. One approach is to feel annoyed or degraded as you clean; the other choice is to be grateful that you have a retail space with a bathroom. Cleaning this room then becomes a privilege enabling you to accept the task willingly.

Be kind to yourself by choosing the productive attitude in accomplishing the necessary, less desirable tasks. Be really kind to yourself by putting a line item in your financial desire list that allows for a cleaning service. Can you imagine how satisfying it will feel to reach this milestone?

As the dates approach, be mindful of completing each action. As we discussed, the dates are important. After each item is completed, remove it from the list and replace the empty line with a new actionable item.

Keep this list posted somewhere that you will see it frequently, perhaps by your desktop or on the bathroom mirror. You could, perhaps, keep it tucked into your pocket and take some time to review it once in awhile. The list is for your benefit and can best serve its purpose if you let it become a natural part of your life.

The next step is even more vital. It is vital because it will act as a mechanism to propel you towards habits that work and away from patterns that were not productive.

Stay committed. Build rewards into your routine to keep motivation high.

Now that your **Long Term Actions List** is complete and you are in possession of a sizable brainstorming list, you will begin to take steps towards completion. Since you will never complete your life's journey until you complete your life's journey, the completion that we are looking towards is the achievement of the financial goals that you have set for yourself.

If you want a bucket of rainwater yet keep the bucket upside down during the rain, it will remain empty and you will not reach your goal. Likewise, if you want to achieve a goal, but do not take any action towards the completion of the goal, you will not reach it. Turn your bucket upright and let the raindrops fill the bucket. Sometimes there will be a lot of rain and other times the drops will be few, but staying steady towards the goal will lead to the results that you want.

One primary benefit of taking inspired or enthusiastic action is that you are increasing the probability of the goal being met, not only through the actions, but also by changing the way you feel about the goal. As the bucket begins to fill, slowly or quickly, it reinforces your belief that the goal is reachable. This reinforcement sends great waves of energy into the universe that are charged with the capability of attracting back that which you desire and believe is possible.

Deadlines

You have your **Long Term Actions List** which contains scattered due dates. Now you will create your **Short Term Actions List**. To begin this program, we will strive to create a two-day list. Consider what actions you can reasonably take over the next two days that will bring you closer to your goals.

Following the same parameters that you followed with the **Long Term Actions List,** construct a list of tasks that can be accomplished over a two-day period. Be pushy, yet reasonable. Strive hard, but be kind. Exaggerate your capabilities, while embracing your limitations. What can you expect to finish within the next two days? Think about your life. Will you be traveling during the next two days? Is one day a weekend day and the other a weekday? Is your social calendar filled? Intense work demands? Kids' activities? Keep a mental agenda and create your list accommodating your life's schedule.

You are the only one who knows whether you are being lenient or demanding.

The number of items you record on your list each time is not dictated. You may have seven items or three. You may decide that the next two days are unusually busy, so you record two tasks. You are the only one who knows whether you are being lenient or demanding with the content. You've got plenty of opportunity to experiment in finding the best balance between structure and fluidity in your list.

Create your list.

Short Term Actions List

Complete the tasks you set forth to complete within the two days allotted. No excuses except for those rare completely unforeseeable circumstances. Not everything that pops up demanding or desiring your attention is a rare, completely unforeseeable circumstance, so don't allow this loophole to give you permission to be too relaxed.

If, suppose, during your first attempt at achieving the **Short Term Actions List** you only got to three out of five items. What do you do? Take this opportunity to redefine what is possible before you create the list for the next two days. As with the **Long Term Actions List,** meeting the self-imposed deadlines is important for many reasons. Try not to falter too much or it will become challenging to recommit with enthusiasm.

Give yourself thirty days using a **Short Term Actions List** with a two-day deadline. Thirty days is the minimum time most people require to make a new pattern a part of their routine. We want for this pattern to become routine.

At the end of thirty days, it's time for some vigorous self-assessment. How did you do with the list? Did you frequently change the items on the list as the time was running out? Did you discover that it was so easy that perhaps you realize your two-day requirements did not push you enough? Did you meet the majority of the deadlines and feel good each time you did? Do you now feel proud of what you accomplished or disappointed in your achievements?

The answers to these questions will determine two things. One – are you ready to create your **Short Term Actions List** less often? Again, only you know for sure. There is no grade at the end of the assignment; the only reward is success. If you are committed, energetically and with enthusiasm, to reaching your financial goals, then you are likely ready to extend the length of your **Short Term Actions List's** deadline.

Review what you have accomplished in the past thirty days. Is it more or less than you imagined you could? Looking back, are you proud? Let these ideas play into your current decision about the frequency of completing your **Short Term Actions List**. For those of you who are proud, enthusiastic, and eager to continue with the underlying wonderful belief that you are closer to your financial goals, change the deadline to three or four days. For those of you who are skeptical or waning in enthusiasm, reconvene with your intention. Why are you reading this book? What do you want? Do you really want what you say you want?

The process should be fun. You will experience pleasure at the thirty day point if, in fact, you actually believe that you can achieve your goals. Watching the accumulation of actions completed should give you a sense of pride and purpose. The pride and purpose will naturally feed your enthusiasm as you continue. You are finally, perhaps for the first time in your life, heading towards total financial freedom. You may also be experiencing for the first time the euphoria enjoyed when purposefully realizing your dreams, all the while knowing that you are directing your own path through your thoughts, actions, and beliefs. That level of control over your life is hugely freeing!

Choose your new timeframe for the completion of the **Short Term Actions List** considering the factors indicated. We recommend that you allot four days to complete the list and give yourself another month with this schedule to realize your success rate with self-discipline, enthusiasm, capability in achieving the tasks, and ability to self-monitor the ease or difficulty in the list requirements.

Quite apparently, the graduation from a two-day to a four-day list will require a more extensive set of requirements indicated on each list. Gearing up for the increased timeframe will take some finesse in adjusting the level of difficulty and quantity of items listed. Also, now that you have been successful at committing to the program for thirty days, can you at this point enthusiastically continue? If you are losing interest or focus, elicit a partner to commit to the program with you. You may have someone you respect and whose opinion you value cheer you on, or you may find someone with goals of their own to partake in their own action plan along side you. Thirty days is an important benchmark, for this moment's attitude usually is predictive of the upcoming outcome. If you are not certain that you can proceed with knowing you are achieving your goals, or with the strength in commitment or enthusiasm to succeed, then change things.

Go back to the beginning of this book and rediscover passages that brought you a sense of empowerment. Reread **THE ANSWERS to your questions about life**. Seek information about how you create your reality with your thoughts and your beliefs. Review your own life's successes and discover why those successes happened. Weren't you doing exactly what this book is asking you do, if not informally? You were focusing on your goal and you were believing that it could happen. That's what it's all about – formally or informally, with a workbook or independently, that's how you generate the success you desire.

All else fails, frankly. While we prefer to put a positive spin on our conversation with you – every now and then it's beneficial to tell it like it is. If you do not believe you can succeed, you will not. So do what it takes now to believe you will succeed and then continue on.

Focus and Commitment

Armed with the knowledge and exercises from this book, what can else you do to increase your ability to attract and maintain wealth? It can be done with a little discipline and steady focus. The final step is to maintain your focus on your goal. By remaining passionate and optimistic about the ability to achieve your goal, you will achieve it. Your passion will guide you towards the steps that will enable your goals to be realized.

Make conscious choices once you feel you understand the direction you should take in working towards your goals. For example, if your goal is to invest profitably in the stock market, and your next step is to seek knowledge to do so, you may do better reading a book entitled, "Easy Ways to Profit in the Stock Market," instead of "The Stock Market and Why it Leads to Financial Destruction of the Individual." This approach seems obvious. Find a mentor. Ask questions of one who has succeeded in the way you want to succeed. Learning from others' success is sometimes more powerful than book learning.

Just as quickly as you learn something new, you tend to disregard it. The nature of being human is to seek new, seek new, seek new. This trait is a great motivator and stimulant for change, but it can also make committing to a plan difficult. If a wonderful idea sparks your interest, how long does it hold your interest? The answer is usually dependent upon how much passion you feel for the idea. A person who wants to skydive is likely to pursue it in proportion to her interest. If it's a mild passing "one day" interest, active steps towards skydiving are not likely to be taken. On the other hand, if the passion behind the desire is great, it's more likely that the steps to succeed at this goal will be taken.

One crossroad that generally separates people with a high level of passion from those with less passion is the tedious steps towards the goal. In every task, there are components of the job that are more fun than others. If, for example, you have to save money for skydiving lessons as your first task, this may be far more dull than having your first lesson. During the monotonous steps, people who feel indifferent towards the overall goal will have a greater dropout rate than those who feel enthusiastic.

Ask questions of one who has succeeded in the way you want to succeed.

You have set financial goals for yourself. We recommend that you plan ways to cheer yourself on during the tedious times. Staying the course is the way to the finish line. Time passes. Time can pass strategically or aimlessly – it's your choice.

The simplest way to help yourself adhere to the tasks when you feel boredom or impatience set in is to create a reward system. If you work for an organization that assigns you a single three-year project, do you not think that the successful completion of the assignment is more likely if the organization encourages your performance during the three years? You want to know that what you do matters. You want confidence that the seemingly meaningless steps have purpose. You want to have validation that staying the course has merit and will lead to the results you desire.

Here's where faith comes in as well. At this point, if you do not believe that the steps outlined in this book will lead to the successful completion of your goals, then you are not very likely to commit to the recommended tasks. If, however, you believe that following this plan will lead to success, then during the times of frustration or impatience, tap into your faith in the plan. Remind yourself why you are doing this and, even if the results are not coming fast enough, stick it out because you know they will arrive.

A reward system can be quite simple. Some people find crossing items off a list reward enough. During the process of meeting your short term goals on your **Short Term Actions List**, the achievement of the tasks may be enough to keep you motivated, but there are other methods that can help as well. First, periodically review several weeks' lists after they are completed. Looking at all you have accomplished over time, things that would not likely have happened without the overall plan, you can be sure to be proud. You can feel a sense of power in what you have done so far.

Review what you have accomplished. Your achievements will renew your commitment.

You might also set up a physical reward system for yourself [and partner, if you have one]. For example, after two weeks of consistently meeting your goals, take time to go see a movie. Get a massage. Go to the beach. Read a book. Buy yourself a latte. Only you know the things that will bring you pleasure. Factor the rewards into your program and it will help you stay committed.

The End

Let's review. You are entitled to all that you desire. You are on earth creating your reality through your thoughts, your beliefs, and your actions. You can use these energies [thoughts, beliefs, and actions] to create your ideal prosperous reality.

Money is one tool on earth that can be used to create your reality. Money itself is not wealth; it is merely a vehicle for the expression of love. Understanding love, or at least the underlying affect that the energy of love has in monetary transactions, will help you improve your power in exchanges with money. The most influential component of love affecting the outcome of monetary transactions is self-love. If you discover that your self-love is weak, strengthening it will strengthen your ability to achieve the result you desire in transactions concerning money.

Following a simple plan will allow you to achieve your financial goals. First, determine what you need. Second, determine what you want. Record your wants in your Ten-List, the exercise from **THE ANSWERS book**, and happily focus on this list three times a day for about five minutes each time.

Commit to the deadlines of your ongoing **Long Term Actions List** and **Short Term Actions List**. The completion of the action plan set forth in the **Short Term Actions List** will bridge the gap between your definition of [and belief in] what you want, and getting it.

Stay committed through partnership, rewards systems, and/or faith. By far, the most important factor in success is believing that it is possible.

Afterward

It's easy to end this book with a wrap-up of the ideas, but we'd prefer to leave you with a broader point to ponder.

Suppose you "got it." Suppose you understood and applied all of the exercises and theories contained within these chapters. What do you think your life would be like? Well, we can tell you for one, you'd be experiencing a new level of freedom. Financial abundance would be automatic – the attainment and the retention of financial wealth would be effortless and everlasting. Not bad.

What is even more powerful than the freedom that you will experience from applying the knowledge within this book effectively is that the wealth you can experience is not limited to financial abundance. As you witness how your thoughts and beliefs, supported by your inspired actions, create your reality, you can recognize that this process applies not only to finances, but also to health and to matters of the heart.

True abundance is success in all three areas. True full wealth is feeling fulfilled in all three areas. True freedom is this success.

On earth there are three primary focal areas in which humans wish to attain fulfillment. These areas are finance, health, and relationships. Your beliefs and consequent actions create your reality in each of these three areas. By succeeding through the guidance of this book, you will have learned how to achieve similar heights in the remaining two areas if you have not already done so.

True abundance is success in all three areas. True full wealth is feeling fulfilled in all three areas. True freedom is this success.

To continue to enlighten you about the mysteries of earth life, we will tell you another important concept about your physical journey. You have learned that money is a vehicle for the expression of love. Your physical body is also a vehicle for the expression of love.

Pure love is the complete absence of negative experience. It is the absolute absence of negative thoughts, beliefs, or feelings. It is bliss. It is radiant.

Your body as a vehicle to express love is not limited to demonstrativeness, sexual experiences, body language, or verbal language; it also encompasses health. Just as money is used to express an ability to give or receive love, the body is used likewise. A body in disharmony is expressing a desire for increased love in one or more areas such as self-love or unconditional love from others. Although the topic of the body as a conduit for love is a book in itself, let it suffice for this concept to be recognized here.

Why does this point matter? Since the third of the three areas of importance in human life is relationships, and relationships are all about the ability to give and receive love, then the first two, wealth and health, must be less significant. Don't misunderstand our use of the word "significant." All three are immensely significant! The third, relationships [including your relationship with yourself], however, is what it's all about. Life on earth and here is all about love. Wealth and health are vehicles for practicing love. Love is all that matters.

The only thing that matters is love.

THE ANSWERS
Continue Your Awakening

What others are saying about Author, Speaker, and Personal & Professional Coach, Karen L. Garvey:

"I wanted to say thank you. After meeting you at the Conference and reading your book, your words continue to encourage my awareness on a daily basis. I have grown exponentially and have been so inspired by your message(s) that they are a permanent influence on my growth. Your book Answers has had the single largest impact on me to date, and for that I thank you." *-Jenny Patterson Israel*

"It was truly wonderful hearing you speak this past weekend. Your stories were fascinating and the tools that you gave us are simple and precise. Thank you so much for sharing yourself with us." *-James A.*

"Karen, you are like a lighthouse standing tall amongst your surroundings and casting a brilliant beacon of white light onto our world. I am grateful that your beam casts it's way to me. Thank you for who you are and what you do." *-Ric Statler*

""Because of her significant business background and experience, Karen is particularly articulate and conversant in a manner that connects well with highly successful people. She skillfully addresses esoteric questions in a comfortable way that listeners can understand and relate to. Karen combines a personal warmth and genuineness with a strong, assured manner that inspires confidence in her abilities. She has made an important contribution to both our guest experience and our business." *- John and Ginny Lopis, Owners, The Lodge at Woodloch Luxury Destination Spa*

"I can't thank you enough for jumping in a little early at our LIRC Conference. Your presentation was outstanding! Everyone loved it! Thanks so much..." *-Lorraine F.*

❖❖❖❖

Additional books by Karen L. Garvey

Begin Here - The Answers To Your Questions About Love & Unconditional Love © 2010; Wyce's Money Book © 2008 [Revised as Money Wisdom © 2013]; The Answers to Your Questions About Life © 2006

For Additional Information and Products:
www.TheAnswersUnlimited.com ❖ Karen@KarenGarvey.com
or call 1.866.263.3879